TRIBAL ALCHEMY

Turning what you have into what you need

By Dave Fleming, PhD

ACKNOWLEDGMENTS

Writing is an interesting dance between the *solitary* and the *communal*. There is no way you can write a book unless you are willing to be solitary, at least to some degree. There is also no way to write a good book unless you allow a community of people to push and pull on your words. I would like to thank the people who pushed and pulled on this book.

Thanks to Sarah Owen, Dawn-Marie Driscoll, John Gamba, Tessa LeSage, Cindy Banyai, and David Fetterman, who provided important and timely insights on content and style. Thanks, Sarah, for encouraging me to stick with this. Thanks to my lovely wife, Jennifer, who also provided insights and support throughout this project (and many others). Thanks to Carolyn Rogers for her just-at-the-right-time input on cover design.

Thanks to Matt Garland at Winning Edits for feedback on the early (and terrible) draft of the book. Thanks to all the people at *Kevin Anderson & Associates* who edited and formatted the book and designed the cover. I am grateful you walked through this process with me.

Finally, thanks to the many people, too numerous to name, who have challenged and sharpened my thinking (over the years) about Tribal Alchemy.

RECOMMENDATIONS

Tribal Alchemy reveals how any organization can use its resources to overcome challenges and seize opportunities—and not just with that overused word "teamwork." If you're looking to increase the consistency and quality of creative solution-making, Fleming's book is a must read.

DAWN-MARIE DRISCOLL
EMERITUS EXECUTIVE FELLOW, CENTER FOR BUSINESS ETHICS, BENTLEY UNIVERSITY

There is something magical about *Tribal Alchemy*. Dave Fleming's writing is engaging and transforming. His ideas force you to reflect on your own organizational practice. He embraces multiple perspectives, invites critique, and presents a recipe for success. *Tribal Alchemy* is not only about groups productively solving problems and creatively producing new answers; it is about the kind of leadership needed if we are to create a better and sustainable future.

DAVID FETTERMAN
PRESIDENT AND CEO, FETTERMAN & ASSOCIATES
PAST PRESIDENT, AMERICAN EVALUATION ASSOCIATION
FORMERLY STANFORD SCHOOL OF MEDICINE

Dave's book isn't just about theory. Dave has been instrumental in moving our company toward a mind-set of creatively overcoming obstacles and seizing opportunities. With his help we are developing proactive, aligned, and collaborative employees who are able to turn what we have into what we need.

SCOTT FISCHER
SCOTT FISCHER ENTERPRISES / HARLEY DAVIDSON MOTOR COMPANY

DEDICATION

To Matt and Drew.

May you find your tribes and know the joy of alchemy.

TABLE OF CONTENTS

SECTION ONE:

What the World Needs Now
is Tribal Alchemy

IT'S THE QUESTION...

Early in the movie *The Matrix*, two of the main characters—Trinity and Neo—meet for the first time. Trinity, one of Neo's soon-to-be mentors and love interest, finds Neo in the corner of a crowded night club. Neo is confused and restless. He is searching for some way to make sense of his one-dimensional existence. Trinity knows this about Neo and approaches him with a confidence that captures his attention. Her next words and actions poke at his complacency.

As the tension heightens between them, Trinity leans into Neo and explains that he is searching for an answer. The answer he searches for, she explains, is wrapped up in a question. Trinity whispers, "It's the question that drives us, Neo. It's the question that brought you here. You know the question, just as I did."

Without hesitation, Neo repeats the question that consumes him. "What is the Matrix?"

This defining moment in the movie reminds us of the power of questions. From time to time, we all have questions that consume us and set us on a path of exploration. Can you think of a question that drives you? Questions push us deeper into uncertainties and curiosities. Big questions do not yield their answers quickly or to the half-hearted seeker. They require time, hard work, and persistence. They drive us, just as they drove Neo to wonder and explore. Little did he know just how life-altering his question would be, how it would set in motion the events that would change . . . everything.

Trinity's simple statements about questions are the right opening ideas for this book, because *this book is also about a question*—one that has driven, and sometimes consumed me, for a long time. It put me on a course that, to this day, shapes my life, as well as my in-the-field work and research. My question isn't about a Matrix, but rather about how humans behave when they ingeniously use what they have to make their world a better place.

The Question That Consumes Me

During times of challenge and opportunity, why do some groups work magic while others don't work at all?

or

Why do some groups ingeniously turn their raw materials into novel and useful outcomes, while other groups remain mindlessly stuck in unproductive actions that stall progress and diminish energy?

This question may seem deceptively simple. However, the insights that emerge from it can help us overcome some of our thorniest challenges and advance promising opportunities.

After 30 years of working with, speaking to, coaching groups of various types, sizes, persuasions, and priorities, this question still prods me every day. It compels me to notice, to listen, to learn, and to share discoveries. As a strategic coach, I've worked with powerhouse groups that were able to *transform challenge into solution* and *opportunity into advantage*. They performed these transformations while facing the same obstacles as their anemic counterparts. Through difficulty and hardship, these solution-making groups *discovered* ways to advance critical goals by ingeniously combining the resources at hand.

I've also observed feeble groups, with all the same external raw materials as their creative counterparts. Yet they routinely squandered resources, whined incessantly, scapegoated, and blamed—all of which led them to a palpable mediocrity, sometimes for years. These groups seemed unable to make much of anything out of their resources. In fact, they usually blamed their ineffective ways on a *lack* of resources.

At a casual glance, the powerhouse and feeble groups appear similar in size, structure, and purpose. But beneath the surface, there are significant differences that lead to their opposing results.

What makes the difference between the two types of groups?

Without knowing you, my hunch is that you've been a part of a powerhouse group. You know firsthand the energy that flows in and out of these groups as they work magic with raw materials. You've experienced the inspiration and satisfaction that surfaced as your group took *what it had* and turned it into *what it needed*.

It's a privilege and a delight to experience these moments, because we want our action to matter when it counts the most. When it does, we are infused with energy, satisfaction, and the joy of forward movement. We also grow weary and frustrated when our groups are stuck in unproductive patterns that diminish the effectiveness of a mission.

Tyler Wang and the Boston Bar That Can

During a recent visit to one of our favorite Boston bars, Audubon Boston, my wife and I talked with the manager, Tyler Wang. Tyler genuinely loves his job. He brims with energy in regards to his knowledge about food and spirits. But his passion goes beyond food and drink. As I sipped my Malbec, Tyler explained that he and his colleagues have a strong desire to *advocate for their guests*. "What does that mean exactly?" I asked as I put my glass down.

"When someone comes in," Tyler explained, "if we don't have what she wants, we show her how we can meet her desire with what we *do* have." I smiled. "Even if we don't have the exact ingredients for a requested drink, we find a way to take *what we have and give her what she hoped for*," Tyler said.

"There *it* is," I thought to myself, sipping the wine with a bit more joy. Tyler continued, "We all work to make that happen for our guests. It means being creative with what's available." His eyes lit up as he talked about the passion and creativity his colleagues employ to delight guests. As Tyler talked, I couldn't help but think of my all-consuming question and a related idea.

The Related Idea

During times of challenge and opportunity, solution-making groups utilize their raw materials—which includes the challenge or opportunity—in very different ways than their feeble counterparts.

This brings us to the purpose of the book: *to explore how groups (tribes) ingeniously transform available resources to overcome challenges and seize opportunities (alchemy).*

Now, I'm not suggesting that effective groups never look for resources beyond their current ones. Of course they do. But they don't view change as solely dependent on acquiring an elusive or missing resource. Instead, they work to arrange what they have, in inventive ways, to meet the demands of what they encounter. The key distinction here is the *object* of the group's collective behavior. *How does the ingenious group behave in relationship to its raw materials during challenge or opportunity*? That's the ticket.

It's also important to point out that this book is *not* primarily about team building. The *purpose* of team building is (primarily) to strengthen various qualities between team members—like trust, cohesion, cooperation, and communication. The goals of team building are usually group health and a basic understanding of how group dynamics affect team performance. That's not the goal of this book—though I'm sure a group that reads this book may experience some increase in health and basic functioning. It's time to put teamwork back where it belongs. Teamwork is the servant of a bigger goal: *collective ingenuity*. How to accomplish that bigger goal is the purpose of this book.

With our purpose in mind, let's go back to the consuming question. We now have a "first" answer (to the question) that will sharpen our exploration.

The Consuming Question

Why do some groups ingeniously turn challenges and opportunities into novel and useful outcomes, while other groups remain mindlessly stuck in unproductive actions that stall progress?

First Answer

Because groups that ingeniously use their resources during challenges and opportunities *behave differently* than do their ineffective counter-parts.

The "first answer" leads us to other questions:

- What exactly occurs when the successful group does its thing?
- Does the inventive group behave in identifiable and repeatable ways?
- Can a group increase ingenious solution making? If so, how?
- Can a feeble group turn it around?

For a moment, recall your participation with both types of groups. What emotions surface as you think about each one?

- Can you think of any behaviors that the powerhouse group regularly exhibited that the feeble one did not?
- Was there a difference in the quality of the work each produced? Describe the difference in specific terms.
- Which type of group would you rather spend your life energy on? Why?

As you read on, keep these two different groups in mind. Relate the ideas in the book to your own experiences. You can use those experiences as case studies to confirm or question my ideas.

The Tribal Alchemy Framework

My obsession with the question of this book led me to create a framework that identifies and increases the behaviors needed to transform your raw materials into creative and useful solutions. I call it *Tribal Alchemy*. Though I created the framework, I certainly did not invent many of the ideas contained in the pages ahead. Tribal Alchemy is supported by ideas and research related to cognitive psychology, neuro-biology, adult development, high-performing teams, as well as emotional and collective intelligence, to name a few. What I have sought to do is ingeniously combine these ideas to provide a pathway for transformation of lesser into better. I'll let you decide if I succeeded. But before we move deeper into the specifics of the framework, let's take a look at Tribal Alchemy in action. *What does it look like when it happens?*

May the question drive you.

WHAT DOES TRIBAL ALCHEMY LOOK LIKE?
Square Peg, Round Hole

We've got to figure out a way to put a square peg in a round hole.

Deep into the Apollo 13 crisis, this iconic mandate was given to a group of NASA engineers. After the initial explosion and mechanical failures, a new threat emerged. The astronauts were in peril due to their own exhalations. They were running out of CO_2 canisters (that collected the gas) for the lunar module. The command module CO_2 canisters were available for use, but with one small problem. The command module connector was square and the lunar module connector was—wait for it—round. Of course it was. Systems experts known as the "Tiger Team" had 24 hours to construct the square-peg-into-round-hole filtration system. Since there was no way to shuttle new parts to the ship, the engineers on the ground had to design a filter using only the materials already on board the spacecraft.

As depicted in the movie *Apollo 13*, the Tiger Team dumped the available materials on a table with these instructions: "The people upstairs have handed us this one and we have to come through. We've got to find a way to make this (holding up a square canister) fit into the hole of this (holding up a round canister) using nothing but that (pointing to the materials on the table)." The final moment of the scene

9

shows the team members organizing their raw materials. You can hear one member say, "Okay, let's build a filter." They did, build a filter, and kept the astronauts breathing long enough to get home.

. . .

There it is, Tribal Alchemy in action. The Tiger Team ingeniously arranged their raw materials, including the challenge itself, to accomplish their objective. Instead of succumbing to defeatist attitudes or actions, they combined raw materials in a way that led to a creative solution. Instead of watching a disaster unfold, they created an inventive solution at *just the right time*. Ed Smylie, the leader of the NASA Tiger Team, reflected in a 2005 Associated Press story, "Apollo 13 turned out to be one of the space program's proudest moments. What could have been a horrible disaster turned out to be a great achievement." The most important word in Smylie's statement is "turned." The disaster "turned out" a certain way because the Tiger Team "turned" (transformed) their raw materials into a creative solution.

The Tiger Team's creative-solution making was not accidental. They may have experienced some luck along the way, but their collective behavior toward the situation increased the likelihood of success. The good news is that these behaviors can be practiced by all kinds of different groups. Your group may not be full of engineers or scientists. You may not create or manufacture products. But the effectiveness of your work increases or decreases somewhat based on *how you behave toward your raw materials during challenges and opportunities*. When you turn your raw materials into something novel and useful, you perform Tribal Alchemy.

Let's take a look at the elements of Tribal Alchemy and how they become a framework for creative solution making.

First, You Need a Tribe

During the writing of my Ph.D. dissertation, I received the following advice from one of my dissertation committee members: "I don't understand why you want to use the word *tribe*. It's just the latest trendy

10

business word that won't be around in a couple of years. If you're going to use it, you should explain why, because it's just not a scholarly idea."

I dedicate this small chapter to that committee member. I also dedicate it to this trendy flash-in-the-pan word, "tribe"—that has been a primal urge of modern humans for 100,000 years or so. I can make this heartfelt dedication because, of course, I've graduated.

I also want to stress that I am using the word *tribe*, and *alchemy* for that matter, as metaphors. I am fully aware that my definition of both words does not match their most literal definitions.

What Is a Tribe and Why Use the Word?

The word *tribe* can create strong reactions, both positive and negative. Some academics and business thinkers use the word to describe collections of people in pursuit of shared goals. Seth Godin popularized the word in his book *Tribes: Why We Need You to Lead Us*. He described a tribe this way: "A tribe is a group of people connected to one another, connected to a leader, and connected to an idea. . . . A group needs only two things to be a tribe: a shared interest and a way to communicate" (p. 1). In their book, *Tribal Leadership: Leveraging Natural Groups to Build a Thriving Organization*, researchers and business thought leaders Dave Logan, John King, and Halee Fischer-Wright used the word to describe naturally forming "small towns" within organizations. These "small towns" possess influence and energy. They have significant influence for good or ill.

Evolutionary biologist Edward O. Wilson took the word *tribe* to a more primal place when he wrote the following in his book *The Meaning of Human Existence* (2014):

> A second diagnostic hereditary trait of human behavior is the overpowering instinctual urge to belong to groups in the first place, shared with most kinds of social animals. . . . A person's membership in his group—his tribe—is a large part of his identity (chapter 3).

It seems that we've been at this tribal-constructing activity (both literally and metaphorically) for quite some time. This is an important point.

Being part of a tribe is not some hip new 21st-century business idea that all the cool kids are talking about. We travel in tribes because, well—we can't help ourselves. It's part of being human. You may think of yourself as a rugged individualist, but, like it or not, you are also tribal.

In my own work and speaking, I've used the word *tribe* for the better part of a decade. I've noticed it resonates with some and seems distasteful to others. Perhaps this is because of the ways in which the word is used—in both positive and negative ways. Some, like those mentioned above, use the word to describe an important human quality that can lead to positive outcomes. However, the word *tribe* has been used to describe narrow-minded group-think that leads to something like "tribal warfare." Others maintain that the world's negative factions are due to "tribalism." Perhaps the word *tribe* produces deep feelings because it is associated with one of our most basic drives, the drive to belong *and to* thrive *as we belong*.

I appreciate the risk in using the word *tribe* in such a central way in this book, and in my work. But I believe the advantages far outweigh the liabilities. We, the human race, are tribal in that we are drawn to others who share similar values, ideas, and interests. We are drawn to others who reinforce our ideas and increase our sense of security and status. We are unlikely to counter evolution in the next, say, 100 years. With that in mind, what we need are tribes that create ingenious solutions to challenges and opportunities and share that power with other tribes, until an ever-growing network makes the world a better place. Of course, this is already happening. We celebrate tribes when we see them performing ingenious actions in the world. We know this kind of tribal collaboration is the answer to many of our woes.

The Tribal Alchemy Variety of Tribes: Narrowing the Definition of Tribe for the Purposes of this Book

Generally speaking, the word *tribe* seems to be used interchangeably with words like *team* or *group*, although *team* and *group* are used far more often in everyday language. At this point, and for a very specific reason, I want to define a "tribe" as a group of people that desire specific outcomes and act to achieve them. This means they share three elements:

- Space—their place of connection
- Desire—their wish for a certain outcome
- Action—their effort to achieve that outcome

In my framework, if you remove any one of those elements, you no longer have a tribe. You may have a group. You may even have a team. But these three qualities are needed to be a tribe in the Tribal Alchemy sense of the word.

As you look at these three elements, you might think all collections of people share these qualities. But pause and reflect a bit deeper and you'll see that many collectives are missing one or more of these elements. If that's the case, they don't have "tribe" status. All three elements must be consistently present in order for a collection of people to be a tribe.

I realize that other people use the word *tribe* in a much more general (or maybe specific) way. I'm sure some would disagree that these three elements must be present in order to attain tribe status. In my framework, the reason all three elements must be present is because *the three elements form the environment in which people can ingeniously use raw materials to transform the world (to perform alchemy)*. No shared space, no possibility for alchemy. No shared desire for specific outcomes, no possibility for alchemy. No shared action to achieve those specific outcomes, no possibility for alchemy. Magic happens when people, either temporarily or for the long haul, become tribal by experiencing all three qualities.

All of the following collections of people *could be tribes*, whether for a few hours or a few years, *if* they share all three elements:

- A duo engaged in a card game
- A board committee charged with identifying the pros and cons of a significant decision
- A collection of people all focused on a work project or initiative
- A group of neighbors who organize a weekly farmers' market

- A group of professionals who organize an association or society to support each other's development

Of course, some of our tribes are more important to us than others. The temporary card-playing duo may not feel as committed to their tribe as, say, the neighbors who organize the farmers' market. However, the reverse could be true as well. It's also likely that some tribes we belong to are more valuable to us because we believe their mission is critical to the well-being of the world.

Think about the various collections of people you are connected to. Which ones rise to tribe status? A few simple questions will help you answer. First, which ones share space? Likely they all do, in some way. Second, which ones are infused with desire for specific outcomes? The desire I refer to here focuses energy and emotion on achievement and also builds positive relational bonds. This energizes people and sustains action. Finally, which ones *work* for shared outcomes? What makes a tribe a tribe is that it *works* for shared outcomes. *If you're not doing something together to advance specific outcomes, you're not a tribe* (in the Tribal Alchemy sense). The reason "working together toward shared outcomes" is critical to tribe status is that it's in the pursuit of shared outcomes that we encounter challenges and opportunities. And it's during those times that we need to ingeniously use our raw materials to transform obstacles and openings.

When you have all three qualities, congratulations, you're a tribe. Now comes the alchemy.

Once You've Got a Tribe, You Need Some Alchemy

A Weird and Wonderful Bunch

History tells the story of a peculiar bunch of people known as alchemists. Among other pursuits, alchemists obsessed over transmutation. Alchemists believed that just the right mixture and manipulation of substances would transform lesser substances (lead) into better ones (gold). Speculations, mythologies, and experimentations abounded in pursuit of that goal. Lead into gold? Seems a bit ridiculous from our view.

What kind of nonsensical pursuit was that? Well, it may not have been all that irrational.

In their book, *Creations of Fire* (1995), Cathy Cobb and Harold Goldwhite wrote, "Alchemists believed in transmutation because they *saw* transmutation everyday of their lives in cooking, dyeing, bodily functions, or producing metals from ores" (p. 30). Cobb and Goldwhite recount a fascinating history of alchemy, which was practiced for more than 1,000 years and influenced the trajectory of what we now know as chemistry. There is no doubt that the ingenious combination of "things" produces other "things." In one sense, the alchemists weren't so far off the mark.

The Wrestling Match

As I picture an ancient alchemist at work in a study, I see a wrestling match between the raw materials and the alchemist. Alchemists manipulated substances in order to unlock the secrets contained within. Whether the raw material was a person or a metal, the goal of the struggle was to transform it into something better. Sound familiar? Kind of like what tribes must do. Alchemy as a metaphor is brilliant and helpful for tribes. As I've already mentioned, alchemy is a tribe's ingenious combination and manipulation of resources (their raw materials) that transforms those raw materials, and corresponding situations, into something better, whatever "better" may be.

Like alchemists, tribe members wrestle with raw materials in order to unlock the potential within situations, circumstances, and objects. The unique mission of your tribe reveals the raw materials you work to transform. Some tribes work with wood or metal or some other substance in order to create an object. Other tribes wrestle with ideas and concepts so they can deliver a service. Others coordinate bodily movements in order to excel at a sport or art form. Many tribes serve people in order to make the lives of those customers or clients better. No matter what your mission or your specific raw materials, Tribal Alchemy occurs when you transform those raw materials into solutions that advance your outcomes (particularly during times of challenge and/or opportunity). Remember, ingenious tribes *behave* a certain way toward their raw materials in order to "alchemize" them and their world.

We have a clearer picture of a basic description of Tribal Alchemy. Now what we need is a way to consistently behave in those ingenious ways that will lead to Tribal Alchemy. We need a simple but robust framework that is usable and repeatable. That's what the Tribal Alchemy framework will do for you. It supplies you with a repeatable alchemy-process for your tribe, as well as a set of practices that *each individual* within your tribe can practice to enhance their personal ability to engage in alchemy. Let's take a look at the framework.

The Tribal Alchemy Framework

What You Stand on Matters

Just outside my Boston apartment are the sounds of renovation. As I look out my window, two different construction crews work diligently on two different houses. Each house is receiving a serious facelift. At the time of writing this chapter, both crews are replacing the exterior siding on their respective house. It's quite a job. Each crew appears to be equipped with skilled workers that have the necessary hand tools and know-how. Each crew has all the necessary materials to remove the old siding and apply the new. Each crew member seems to get along with his fellow crew members. Both crews work long hours—beginning early in the morning and staying throughout the entire day. However, one crew has an enormous advantage.

Crew A—let's call them the *disadvantaged crew*—uses ladders to position themselves along the wall. Here's what it looks like to be Crew A. A crew member leans the ladder against the wall. He then climbs up the ladder and loosens some of the old siding. Then he climbs back down the ladder and moves it a foot or so to the right or left. He then climbs back up the ladder and loosens a bit more of the siding. Then, back down the ladder he goes, moving the ladder another foot as he works another section of the wall. He makes this move over and over and over. Mind you, we are talking about a significant part of an exterior wall of a three-story house, and the siding covers a large portion of that wall. Not only does the crew member continuously move the ladder, but he also must work on different rungs to reach different sections of the wall. I'm just an observer and my back hurts.

Crew B has it all over Crew A. Let's call Crew B, the *scaffolders*. If their name doesn't give it away, Crew B has a scaffold. It's just not a fair fight between Crews A and B. Crew B positions planks on the frame of the scaffold and then stands on those planks to reach large sections of the wall in a fraction of time. Don't get me wrong: it's still a lot of work, even with the scaffold. But the advantage is significant. Not to mention that Crew B leaves the scaffold in place and returns the next day ready to go. It's a support that enhances progress, not to mention increasing happiness.

There are many types of scaffolding that support various actions in the world. Another word for a scaffold is *a framework*. The structure changes depending on the application, but generally speaking, a framework is a support system that makes other work easier, quicker, and more effective. It eases the burden of certain elements of a job, enabling focus on another, more important part (like applying siding). Frameworks are genius.

For example, web application frameworks are essential for computer programmers because they support the development of applications and other web resources. The Wikipedia definition notes that a framework "aims to alleviate the overhead associated with common activities performed in web development." This description highlights the fact that frameworks "handle" certain elements of development so that the programmer can save time and create at a higher level. If a programmer had to redesign basic elements of websites every time she created one, it would be an enormous waste of time—just like the ladder is an inefficient way to replace siding on a wall.

Frameworks support and ease the burden of certain parts of a job or action so that we can focus on more important or higher level elements— like making alchemy.

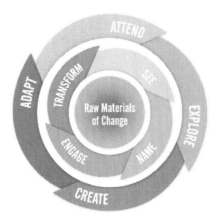

THE FRAMEWORK OF TRIBAL ALCHEMY

The Tribal Alchemy framework reveals and explores the actions that alchemy-producing tribes employ with their raw materials during times of challenge and opportunity. It is a flexible and repeatable framework that has three basic elements.

Element Number One: Raw Materials

The first element is your raw materials, and a specific mind-set your group must cultivate around those raw materials. Your raw materials are a combination of your tribe's knowledge, objects, tools, and resources combined with your challenges and/or opportunities.

Element Number Two: The Process of Tribal Alchemy

The process of Tribal Alchemy highlights four dynamic and interrelated steps that tribes repeat in order to alchemize. The four steps are: see, name, engage, and transform.

See: Circle around and see into your raw materials. Notice, reflect, and describe. Do this through the art of question making, perspective taking, and a specific kind of collective conversation.

Name: Give the challenge or opportunity you face a name. Naming increases its value, ownership, and accountability. Naming also creates a frame that will guide the alchemy. The name and the frame should reflect the challenge/opportunity in a very specific manner.

Engage: Together, emotionally embrace and strategically utilize both raw materials and the genius of the tribe to explore transformative solutions. Be emotionally engaged and watch for moments of insight that reveal possibilities.

Transform: Together, make the solution concrete through action. Risk forward in order to manifest the better way. Learn from the alchemy process in order to create even better alchemy in the future. Celebrate the alchemy in order to increase collective energy and camaraderie.

Element Number Three: Member Practices

The third element of the framework is a set of practices individual tribe members practice to stay *alchemy-ready*. It's hard to have a tribe of alchemists if the individuals in that tribe are not behaving in ingenious ways. The four practices are:

Attend: Pay attention to self, others, and situations.

Explore: Be curious and discovery-centered.

Create: Be creative in your life and work.

Adapt: Graciously flex with change.

Your tribe is likely already executing elements of the framework. The aim is to use it with increasing mindfulness and consistency. That's when your tribe will turbocharge alchemy.

The Sections of the Book

The second section of the book explores the unique role challenge and opportunity play in the pursuit of alchemy. Section three explores the process of alchemy and how to use each step more effectively within your tribe. Finally, section four highlights the individual member practices that enhance each member's ability to contribute to the tribe's alchemy (they are also not a bad way to live your life). I've watched this framework in action for the better part of three decades. Even before I arranged it into its current form, I noticed the elements at work within alchemy-creating tribes. I am confident that these elements can enhance your tribe's alchemy and encourage you to read it together (if you're small enough) or in small clusters (if you're a big tribe) in order to practice alchemy even in your reading and reflections.

SECTION TWO:

Wrestling Down Your Tribe's Raw Materials

Raw Materials of Change

A common tactic, for instance, was to try to make a material appear more godlike, on the theory that if it assumed enough of the qualities of gold, it would eventually be gold—not an unreasonable approach. As was common to all the approaches, the methods used included distillation, sublimation (transforming a heated solid into a gas with no liquid phase), fusion (melting), solvation (dissolving), filtration, crystallization, and calcination (heating to a high temperature without melting; this usually results in oxidation—incorporating oxygen from the air).

Creations of Fire (1995), p. 35

For alchemists, the goal of transmutation varied. Most often it was the production of gold, although it could be medicine or even transmuting old into young or earthy body into soul. The techniques of transmutation also varied: Some alchemists took a pragmatic approach, dissolving, melting, combining, distilling, but others used only magic incantation. Most used both.

Creations of Fire (1995), p. 30

What's on Your Table?

At the beginning of the *Apollo 13* "build-a-filter" scene, the Tiger Team enters the room to receive instructions. An engineer dumps the usable materials onto a table. The random pieces scatter and are in need of alchemy. As the Tiger Team encircles "the mess," the directives are given. What appear to be random and disconnected materials await a tribal transformation. The scene ends as the engineers organize the elements to see what they've got.

When challenges and opportunities emerge, unknowns and ambiguities come along for the ride. At the outset of a challenge or opportunity, chaos and uncertainty are traveling mates (actually they travel with us most of the time). This means that a tribe must initiate the work of alchemy *in the midst* of the ambiguity, without knowing where it will all lead. Without this movement-into-the-mess, there can be no alchemy. I get energized by these unnerving moments because I know the possibility of transformation is hiding inside. There is no doubt that these moments can be frustrating and disorienting, but when the raw materials are lying on the table, resourceful tribes lean in.

This same chaotic moment occurs for your tribe, maybe multiple times a day. You too face challenges and opportunities that require transformation. The raw material of situations, objects, and people scatter across your "table." Your tribe must harness ingenuity and creatively combine raw materials into needed solutions. *This is the beginning of alchemy.*

Alchemy begins when a tribe perceives their raw materials in a specific way.

The framework of Tribal Alchemy is only useful if a tribe views challenges and opportunities as *positive invitations for change*. Failure to alchemize is often due to unproductive mind-sets and attitudes that arise alongside difficulty or opportunity. Too often tribe members view a challenge as an irritation that breeds negative generalizations, like *things will never change,* or *this is so unfair,* or *here we go again,* or *great, just what we need right now.* This attitude toward challenge eliminates the possibility of alchemy. Passion for transformation wanes.

Tribe members can also have unproductive mind-sets around opportunities. Some view opportunities as "shiny objects" that divert attention from important work. Some recoil from change as if it's a disease. Still others pin the future on one opportunity because they don't want to do the hard work that would lead to sustainable effectiveness. Many tribal leaders are quick to turn opportunity into the next "big thing" that will make every other thing better. This can lead tribe members to diminish genuine opportunity because failed attempts of the past create skepticism about the future. This tribal dance—between leaders and people—eliminates the possibility of alchemy more times than tribes realize. I've watched the sabotage and frustration from both leaders and people ruin great strategic possibilities.

When it comes to your tribe's raw materials, collective attitude matters.
If that's amiss, the potential for alchemy is downgraded.

Early Detection of Alchemy: Challenge and Opportunity

If challenge or opportunity had a voice they would say, "Hey tribe, it's time. Heads up. This situation is ripe for creative magic making. Be awake, be mindful, and of course, get ready to practice alchemy." Instead of viewing challenges and opportunities as impediments or dreams for someday, they are cues and clues that the potential for alchemy is near. You can't alchemize if you don't know the situation is ripe for it. When challenge and opportunity emerge, your tribe must activate.

Make a Shift

Move from

Challenge as difficulty that blocks progress and frustrates the tribe

to

Challenge as invitation to rearrange raw materials in order to overcome barriers and advance the mission and the capacity of the tribe

. . .

Move from

Opportunity as potential dream for the future

to

Opportunity as "revealer" of the changes that must occur in order to create a better future

Let's take a closer look at both challenge and opportunity and why they matter so much to alchemy.

Why Does Challenge Signal and Inspire Alchemy?

In the movie *Pleasantville*, two teenagers from the 1990s are transported through their television back to the 1950s. What David and his sister Jennifer discover (in this made-up TV land) is a *Leave It to Beaver*–like world where everyone and everything is perfect. Troubles don't exist. Life is easy and simple and always goes to plan. Basketballs always find the basket. Geography lessons are simple because the size of the town and the size of the world are one and the same. The roads lead residents back to where they started. It's all very pleasant. But something is wrong.

As David and Jennifer get to know the townspeople, a painful fact emerges. Though everyone in Pleasantville is pleasant indeed, this quality makes them, and the town itself, boring and bland. There is no advancement of anything. The pleasant life is void of texture, meaning, and purpose. In fact, everyone and everything—the entire world of Pleasantville—shows up in black and white. There is no color. Why? Color, as the residents of Pleasantville come to understand, is the result of creativity, ingenuity, passion, and risk. As David and his sister introduce these and other qualities to townspeople, they take on color; they take on life. Because of this, a division evolves for the first time in the town's pleasant history. The townspeople split; some choose to embrace challenge, and some hold on to predictability.

Pleasantville reminds us that *life gets better as it gets harder. We need life to be hard.* Challenges make alchemy possible. These barriers to advancement inspire us to overcome through ingenuity. We know that even our brains need challenge in order to thrive. The late Lawrence Katz, a neurobiologist at the Howard Hughes Medical Institute, conducted research on the brain. He determined that the brain needs exercise in a similar way as the rest of our body. He was instrumental in the creation of neurobics—everyday ways you can exercise your brain. Since Katz wrote his book in 1999, a mountain of research confirms the need to challenge the brain through a variety of training and exercise methodologies. It seems that our brains thrive on challenges because challenges require the brain to work hard for specific rewards. Tribal (collective) brains are the same. Challenges must be overcome, and that requires alchemy. Tribes that push deep into these challenges, even when those challenges are hard, are the ones that work and live in color.

No challenges, no new ideas

No challenges, no change in action or condition

No challenges, no meaning

As much as we thrive on challenges, we often complain about the very dynamic (challenge) that enables advancement. I find this an interesting characteristic of our biology and social interactions. We seem to dislike the challenges necessary for advancement. Even though we know that advancement comes through challenge, we still fight it. We resist that which moves us forward.

Take a personal example. I've run, as part of my exercise regimen, for the better part of 20 years. To this day, as soon as I begin a run, I usually have two thoughts:

1. I should stop immediately.
2. I'm going to die.

The irony is, I know all the benefits that come from this type of exercise, and I experience them on a regular basis. And still, I resist. Why? What's going on here?

Mihaly Csikszentmihalyi suggested a reason for this resistance. A renowned psychologist who researches the qualities of optimal experiences, which he calls Flow, Csikszentmihalyi suggested that though we have an urge to create, we resist the creative urge because of a stronger competing urge. In his book *Creativity: Flow and the Psychology of Discovery and Invention*, he wrote the following:

> Another force that motivates us, and it is more primitive than the urge to create: the force of entropy. This too is a survival mechanism built into our genes by evolution. It gives us pleasure when we are comfortable, when we relax, when we can get away with feeling good without expending energy. (p. 109)

Yep, that pretty much sums it up. Let's face it, there's something particularly appealing about *Pleasantville*. In the struggle of a day, we may confess our desire for a path of zero resistance. Maybe even just less resistance would do. We feel thwarted by unforeseen circumstances or annoying people sent to derail our forward movement. I don't know about you, but I wouldn't mind if all my basketball shots found the hoop. I wouldn't mind if the work of my tribes were met with cheers from adulating fans. But alas, this is not the case. And, of course, it's good that it's not.

Through his research, Csikszentmihalyi identified conditions necessary for ingenuity and creativity. What he found only confirms the essential role of challenge.

The conditions of flow include:

- Perceived challenges or opportunities for action [the raw materials of alchemy].
- Clear goals and immediate feedback about the progress that is being made.

(*Flow and the Foundations of Positive Psychology,* 2014, p. 240.)

There are, of course, limits to the value of challenge. Take weightlifting for example. Just add an extra 100 pounds to any part of your normal routine and you will find the limits. Too much challenge overwhelms us. But equally, too little struggle and we grow lazy and lethargic. Just decrease your weight training by 50 pounds or more and see what happens. Without the right amount of struggle, it seems we zone out or burn out. Goldilocks is alive in all of us.

I purposely left out a critical portion (above) from Csikszentmihalyi's first condition of Flow. Here's the entire sentence:

Perceived challenges, or opportunities for action that stretch (neither overmatching nor underutilizing) existing skills; a sense that one is engaging challenges at a level appropriate to one's capacities.

So . . .

Where the Alchemy Lies

Too Little Struggle		Too Much Struggle
(Lethargic, Apathetic)	**X**	(Overwhelmed, Paralyzed)

When challenge overwhelms, entropy beckons us to "take it easy." When there's too little challenge, a sense of meaninglessness prods us to get with it. When challenge is appropriate in scope and meaningful to shared outcomes, it highlights the need for alchemy and inspires tribes to go after it. *Learning to read this moment of challenge-to-alchemy is a skill of great value.* The good news is that there is a tried and true indicator that your tribe is close to a challenge that is in need of alchemy. You'll never guess what it is.

. . .

One way to spot a challenge is to listen to the conversations of a tribe. When challenges arise, there is often tribal angst that runs parallel to the challenge. Tribal angst surfaces within interactions. At some point, it's likely that this talk will turn to complaining. When situations or circumstances are difficult, it feels natural to complain. It may be more natural than we even know. However, not all complaining is created equal. Tribes engage in the same two types of complaints as individuals. Think about how you complain as an individual. Some complaints lead to apathy and some to alchemy.

Neuroscientists have discovered that when we perceive a task as hard, it fires up a part of the brain normally associated with pain or anxiety. Since most of us want to avoid pain, complaining about it is a good first step. Back to running and my longtime angst with it. When faced with a challenging run, my desire for entropy kicks in. It's no wonder then that my negative mind-set is lurking nearby as well. Along with this distasteful mind-set, something else emerges as I run. Complaints. I inwardly protest and catalog a litany of issues, including physical ones, that are obstacles to my goal. Here are a few of my favorites:

- It's hot.
- It's cold.
- It's perfect outside and I still suck.
- If my legs were longer . . .
- All these people on the streets are messing up my pace.
- I'll never get the results others get.
- Are you kidding me, I miss one week of running and the next time I run I get a cramp. Really?

I could go on, but you get the point. The complaints above have never once created better outcomes for me. This doesn't mean, though, that all complaining is negative or counterproductive. Through my love-hate affair with complaining while running, I've learned there is a type of complaining that can lead to better results. Here are a few examples:

- Why in the world do I keep running out of energy halfway through my run?
- Oh great, I'm getting shin pain.
- That was my 5K time? That's terrible.
- I hate that my legs hurt every time I run over six miles.

What is the difference between the two types of complaining? Part of the difference has to do with where the complaining takes me *after I make the complaint.* Does it lead to apathy or alchemy? This is true for tribes as well. During challenges, it's common for tribe members to complain. That complaining can lead toward or away from alchemy. Tribal complaining may actually be unavoidable; it may be part of our collective makeup. If this is the case, complaining then isn't the issue. What's important with regard to complaining is what happens after it occurs. Tribes must choose the step *after* complaining with wisdom because it *sets them up* for either apathy or alchemy. Let's take a look at two types of complaining and why one leads toward and the other away from alchemy.

Type One: Unproductive Complaining

Unproductive complaining has a powerful effect on tribes. It grinds joy and engagement into small little pieces and sweeps them into the trash. The goals of Type One complaining include a fortification against change, an escape from responsibility, or an obliteration of progress. In other words, the goal is to quash alchemy. This complaining is often accompanied by a foul mood of some sort. There is no desire to take the challenge and make magic because that would end the need for complaining.

Type One complainers complain because they've found it to be a useful strategy for self- or group preservation. The complainer has no desire to do anything other than be mad or frustrated and take that anger out on anyone nearby. This kind of complaining zaps energy and breeds discontent. There is no progress because the entire purpose of the complaining is to welcome entropy. The complainer roams around in dead-end thoughts and feelings.

In my work, I've noticed that most people mishandle complaints. Here are four types of mishandled behaviors that occur during Type One complaining.

Mishandler One: The Perpetrator

The perpetrator is the source of complaining. She initiates it due to frustration. The perpetrator works hard to draw people into the circle. She is often hurt, tired, burned out, or worse. The perpetrator is unhappy about, well, most everything going on in the tribe and looks to blame and scapegoat.

Mishandler Two: The Perpetuator

The perpetuator fans the flames with timely negative comments and the creation of allies to support the un-happiness. However, he works hard to avoid being seen as the perpetrator. He wants to ride the middle line, not appearing to take sides but enjoying the feelings associated with blame and lethargy.

Mishandler Three: The Avoider

The avoider doesn't participate in the gossip because she believes it's a waste of time and leads to nothing but trouble. However, the passive nature of the avoider allows the dysfunction to continue unencumbered. In the name of "staying out of it," she enables the furtherance of unproductive complaining.

Mishandler Four: The Denier

The denier is a specific type of avoider. The mantra of the denier is "everything is just great." Or, "Oh I just don't focus on that stuff. I'm just positive and things aren't really that bad anyway." The denier enables the dysfunction through a rose-colored and distorted view of the situation.

The four types of mishandlers reveal the tribal nature of unproductive complaining. One or two people on a tribe may be the perpetrators of complaining, but other tribal behaviors enable the complaining to root itself in the psyche of the tribe. Learning to overcome these behaviors is tribal as much as it is individual. Tribe members feed off each other and set off a chain reaction of unproductive complaining that weakens desire to alchemize.

Type Two: Productive Complaining

Productive complaining has a purpose, and that purpose is alchemy. Productive complaining occurs when the complaining highlights something that is wrong in the system, something that needs to change. The issue can be frustrating and even cause tribe members to express frustration. But the difference between unproductive and productive complaining is the *purpose*. Productive complaining reveals the issue in order to free the tribe from a problem through solution making. It's kind of like productive coughing. When my sons were young and sick, the doctor would often encourage what she called "productive coughing." The coughing gets gunk out that is slowing the healing process. Once the gunk is out, the body can go back to magic making. Though it was always hard to let them cough, in certain cases, it was exactly what needed to occur.

The word *complain* comes from the French word *complaindre*. This word literally meant to beat the breast in grief. Over time, the word became associated with the grief of physical pain. We still use the word in this manner even today. If I said to you, "I went for a run and my legs complained the entire time," you would understand that my legs hurt during the run.

When tribe members complain, it's likely that there is "pain" somewhere in the work or the system. As we've seen, some people have made a sport out of complaining. They don't complain to locate challenges that need alchemy but rather to thwart progress or find solidarity with other serial complainers. This is not productive complaining and should be eliminated from tribal communication. Productive complainers identify challenges and then quickly initiate alchemy to address them. The speed with which tribe members move from complaining to creating alchemic solutions is another way to determine if the complaining is productive. I'm not sure we can get rid of all complaining. I'm not even sure we should. What we want to rid our tribes of is endless complaining about the same things.

Faye Crosby (1993) in a journal article entitled "Why Complain?" put it this way:

> Silence without end is not acceptable. There is cause for grumbling and a need for action. Working for a better world is a task fraught with constant difficulties. The very first challenge—the one that must be met if the long, hard work of social action is to meet with success—is to assert one's point of view honestly and without pretense. To do so requires the courage to initiate action long before one is strong enough to win a confrontation and the wisdom to sustain the action in face of a frank realization that one is annoying or inconvenient to others who are as human and as good as oneself. (p. 175)

34

Ingenious tribes make room for productive complaining. We have ways of describing this productive complaining that sets it apart as positive. In my work with tribes, I've noticed they often use the word *pushback* to indicate a desire to complain or challenge the prevailing idea. Too often leaders squelch complaining because either the tribe is stuck in unproductive complaining or because the leader is threatened by the mere idea that someone would be "disloyal" enough to counter or protest. Smart tribes know that productive complaining not only reveals challenges in need of alchemy but is the signal that action, or alchemy, is needed.

Again, Crosby wrote:

> First, when complaining, we should remember that protest is but the first of many steps in making a better world. Actions, which may or may not be accompanied by more complaints, are integral to the meliorative enterprise. Neither at the level of interpersonal face-to-face relationships nor at the level of societal interactions is it healthful and helpful to complain chronically "without offering solutions to problems." Complaint without action is ultimately unsatisfactory. (p. 170)

One of the significant differences between productive and unproductive complaining is delivery. Oftentimes productive complaining is delivered with an "I've got our back" or "heads up" approach. However, there are times that irritating people, who deliver their complaints in irritating ways, have productive insights. In this case, we have to get past the delivery in order to discern the nugget of insight. We also should do more to encourage people to diminish irritating styles of delivery. We will talk more about individual accountabilities in the "practices" section.

What's important at this point is to understand that complaining often reveals challenge, and challenge reveals the possibility of alchemy. Second, tribes have the benefit of dealing with complaints together—if it's productive, that is. They can attend and absorb together. Complaining must lead toward creative solutions and away from entropy. Tribe members can more easily push through this entropy and embrace the barriers that invite ingenuity and progress—that is, if they are mindful. If tribes are mindless, then complaining is the first step toward entrenchment and entropy. This eliminates creative thinking and a desire to work for alchemy.

Tribes turn challenge into something negative when they taint the challenge with bad attitudes. Tribes turn challenge into something positive when they inspire each other to overcome. This is why *the way* tribes engage challenge and each other *in the moment of challenge* is critical—something we will explore in the process of alchemy.

Opportunity Is Running

The ancient Greeks had two words to describe the concept of time. The first was *chronos*, which described the "passing of time." Words like chronometer and chronology come from the word *chronos*. The second word, *kairos*, is my favorite word in the world of words. *Kairos* described a moment when time intersected with opportunity. *Kairos* time beckoned a person or group to make an idea or possibility tangible in the concrete world. If we understand some of the history behind the word, it provides us with a great picture of both opportunity and our interplay with it.

In Greek mythology, Kairos was the youngest son of Zeus. He was good-looking and moved quickly on his tiptoes, which made him hard to catch. Kairos was also bald except for a tuft of hair falling over his eyes. The best way to catch him was to keep him in front of you so you could grab his tuft of hair. Once he passed by you, because he was fast and bald, your chances of capturing Kairos greatly diminished. What a great way to describe opportunity. When opportunity is in front of us it's easier to catch. Once it's passed, it's much harder and causes us to feel regret. The ability to seize opportunity at the appropriate time is a tribal skill to cultivate.

. . .

At our house we have a cat named Kiki that perfectly understands the *kairos* moment. To say that Kiki is fond of a good firm brushing is to woefully understate the obvious. Kiki pretty much lives to eat and be brushed. I have become the favorite brusher, which is ironic on many levels. Here's how the drill goes. Kiki stands in the hallway waiting to make eye contact with me. As soon as I turn toward her and our eyes meet, she begins to whine. If I continue to walk toward her, she runs ahead of me toward the bedroom where the brush lays on the bed. If I enter the bedroom, she's pretty sure the planets have aligned. She hops on the bed and looks at me with "what are you waiting for" eyes. The process with Kiki begins when she sees me coming. That is the essence of *kairos*, and of opportunity. Seize it while it's in front of you because once it passes it's a lot harder to catch.

Kairos moments can be big or small. They can redirect the entire trajectory of life or enhance a single moment in time. They are opportunities in waiting. But *kairos* moments are more than that. They are invitations calling out to you and your tribe. They are invitations to notice what is happening (or what is not happening) and then use your tribal skills of alchemy to create or enhance. Like challenges, opportunities signal the need for alchemy. When we see *kairos* running toward us, we have a limited time to "make something" of the opportunity.

The emergence of opportunity is a delicate moment for a tribe. Not everyone will see the opportunity the same way. Some may not even want to pursue it. Others may see it as the most important possibility in years. Learning how to look together at the opportunity is critical to determining next steps. If the tribe's focus is derailed by competing or selfish agendas, determining how to proceed is clouded by misaligned values or ideas. Achieving a common agenda increases the potential of wise decision making and leads to better alchemy. When a tribe sees opportunity as a moment to change the world and achieve common outcomes, the possibility of alchemy increases. Shared outcomes matter because they have the power to align the action of alchemy. When tribes lose a common agenda, they splinter off and diminish the power of their collective behavior.

Ironically, as important as common outcomes are, if you focus too much on achieving them, your tribe could spoil the energy of opportunity.

You have to stay flexible and open to what emerges along the way. In order to do this, when opportunity runs toward your tribe and you determine it's time to alchemize, catch it and then focus on *executing your alchemy with excellence*. Don't get enamored with what the opportunity might yield for you—like money, fame, or power—or you could lose it all. When a tribe focuses on execution of alchemy—during an opportunity—it increases the possibility of alchemy and increases its skills at performing alchemy.

. . .

Far more in-depth examinations of challenge and opportunity exist in both books and research. The purpose here is to think about the tribal mind-sets that increase or decrease the potential for alchemy. Your tribe's ability to work the process of alchemy is dependent on its view of its raw materials. The way you view challenge and opportunity has a lot to do with whether you can make any magic out of them. And with that, we've arrived at the process of alchemy. We're ready to explore the actions that tribes execute—sometimes in sequence and often in a mash-up—that enable alchemy.

SECTION THREE:

The Tribal Alchemy Process

SEE

More than Dots

Occasionally I get obsessed with autostereograms. With a quick Google search, you can read about autostereograms and take a look at examples. Even if the name doesn't ring a bell, I'm sure you've seen these pictures. When you first look at an autostereogram, it appears to be nothing more than a random series of dots. If, however, you stare in a particular way, the random dots suddenly organize and transform into an amazing 3-D picture. Jacques Ninio, in his 2007 journal article "The science and craft of autostereograms," noted that autostereograms "spread all over the world in 1992–1994, and these images, it was claimed, opened a new era of stereoscopic art" (from the abstract).

I remember the first time I saw an autostereogram. I was so intrigued with the transformation that occurred when I looked the right way. To this day, I love to stare at them and wait for 3-D picture to pop out at me. The revelation of the picture is an exhilarating moment. It seems to happen when I have a kind of focusing-but-letting-go-gaze that allows something else to emerge. It usually takes me a few moments to get my eyes, and my psyche, ready to see more than dots. But it is always worth the wait.

Become a Tribe of Seers

The act of staring at and anticipating a picture hidden in the dots is a great way to describe the first process step of Tribal Alchemy. In order to leverage the potential of challenge and opportunity, tribes must stare together at what often appears to be nothing more than random dots. But if tribes stay with it (keep looking together), the dots eventually "pop" and the potential reveals itself. It's a moment of collective insight that holds great power and promise. What appear to be scattered ideas or objects organize in new ways through the observations and conversations of the tribe.

If tribes want to move beyond the scattered surface to find what is hidden in their raw materials, they must become *seers*. For me, the word seer has a double meaning. On the one hand, the word means to see what is in front of us, as in seer. This is not always easy to do with the dots in the way. On the other hand, the seer, in some ancient cultures, was a person who could look into situations as well as the future and, from that vision, suggest a course of action in the present. Michael Flower, professor of classics at Princeton University, described a seer in his book *The Seer in Ancient Greece* (2008):

> Their competence was exceptionally broad, encompassing all of the various forms of divination that are found in our literary sources. The methods include the interoperation of the movements, behavior and cries of birds (augury) and the interpretation of dreams and of portents (such as lightening, thunder, earthquakes, eclipses, and any other unusual occurrences). The seer also examined the entrails of a sacrificial animal for marks and abnormalities of various kinds (extispicy), as well as interpreting the results of burning the entrails (empyromancy). (p. 24)

41

Of course, I'm not suggesting tribe members learn to read the entrails of a sacrificed animal—although that could really spice up your meetings. Then what is it about the ancient seer that tribe members should emulate? If you look at Flower's description, the seer *looked into things* in order to *perceive* what was hidden within. He or she peered beyond the surface of raw materials to find important messages or realities. In a sense, this is exactly what tribes do when they peer into their raw materials. They look beyond the surface of the dots—the raw materials—lying on the table and think together about *what could be*. They ask questions like, How could the raw materials be rearranged? How could we use what we have in new ways? What do we see beyond the obvious? This seeing together often initiates alchemy and supports the entire experience of change.

Seeing Isn't Just about Seeing

Ironically, seeing together is as much about what we *don't see* as it is about what we do. Chris Chabris and Daniel Simons put themselves on the map with their research on everyday illusions. In their most well-known study, "Gorillas in Our Midst" (1999), Chabris and Simons gathered a few students and created a simple but compelling video. The video shows two groups of students passing basketballs. One group is wearing black shirts and the other white. The simple instructions given, prior to the beginning of the video, ask observers to count the number of passes the team wearing white shirts makes during the duration of the video. Of course, counting the number of passes is only one part of the experiment. About halfway through the video, a gorilla slowly walks onto center stage, carries on a bit, and walks off. The astonishing fact is that around 50% of observers do not see the gorilla because their focus is on counting basketballs. The experiment reveals that individuals sometimes can't see what *seems* apparent. Chabris and Simon name this phenomenon inattentional blindness. They described it this way:

> This name distinguishes it from forms of blindness resulting from a damaged visual system; here, people don't see the gorilla, but not because of a problem with their eyes. When

people devote their attention to a particular area or aspect of their visual world, they tend not to notice unexpected objects, even when those unexpected objects are salient, potentially important, and apparently right where they are looking. (p. 6)

And again they wrote,

In this chapter, when we talk about looking, as in "looking without seeing," we don't mean anything abstract, vague or metaphorical. We literally mean looking right at something. (p. 13)

Though Chabris and Simon's work focused on physical eyesight, other types of perception are susceptible to inattentional blindness as well (we miss insights, ideas, and solutions staring us in the face). Individual tribe members often overlook elements contained within challenge as well as possibilities hidden within opportunity, not to mention potential strategies for alchemy. *No one person can see all the angles of a challenge or opportunity*. Seeing is tribal as much as it is individual. It's why each member must become a seer. Only when they work together, though, will the vision lead to alchemy.

Cathy Davidson enhanced the metaphorical and tribal view of inattentional blindness in her book, *Now You See It: How Technology and Science Will Transform Schools and Business for the 21st Century*. Davidson suggested that individual inattentional blindness might have significant value. A tribe's collective view of circumstances, situations, challenges, and opportunities creates a more rounded view. She wrote, "For the last decade, I've been exploring effective ways that we can make use of one another's blind spots so that, collectively, we have the best chance of success" (p. 5).

Together, people have the potential to create a better view of the complexities of their environment and circumstances. Davidson continued, "If we see selectively, but we don't all select the same things to see, that also means we don't all miss the same things" (p. 2). Here is the power of tribal seeing. The ability to learn from selective seeing requires a tribe to ask questions of each other and embrace, rather than recoil from, multiple perspectives.

Seeing together is about perceiving the ambiguities contained in the challenge and opportunity. Seeing together requires active observation of *what is* and an active imagination about *what could be*. Perceiving challenges and opportunities and imagining possibilities is a type of collective mindfulness that readies the tribe for magic making. Let's take a closer look at the mindfulness that allows a tribe to see together.

Open Your Eyes

For decades, researcher and professor Karl Weick and his colleagues have explored "high reliability." When groups of people perform high-stakes, even dangerous, activities in consistently successful ways, they have high reliability. Just think about it. If a group executes dangerous activities, they obviously don't want to make mistakes. If a surgical team makes a mistake, or personnel on an aircraft carrier get careless, the consequences can be devastating. Weick and colleagues named these high-stakes organizations "high reliability organizations" because ongoing reliability is critical to their success.

In the 1990s, Weick and Karlene Johnson observed the behavior of personnel on an aircraft carrier. From that work, they coined the term "heedful interrelating." Heedful interrelating occurs when a group remains mindful (heedfully relating) about their collective behavior *as they work*. This group mindfulness reduces the number of errors that occur. Here's how Weick and Johnson put it in their journal article, *Collective Minds in Organizations: Heedful Interrelating on Flight Decks*: "Collective mind is manifest when individuals construct mutually shared fields. The collective mind that emerges during the interrelating of an activity system is more developed and more capable of intelligent action the more heedfully that interrelating is done" (p. 365).

In the case of Tribal Alchemy, heedful interrelating is about the *quality* of attention (and eventually action) the tribe directs toward its challenges and opportunities. As we've seen, the dysfunctional tribe doesn't appreciate how its members' attention and behavior *toward challenges and*

44

opportunities affects their outcomes. Weick has evidence that collective mindfulness about behavior leads to a reduction of errors. However, could the practice of group mindfulness be taken further? Could heedful interrelating also enable a tribe to *overcome* challenges and *seize* opportunities? According to Weick and Kathleen Sutcliffe, the answer is yes. In *Managing the Unexpected* (2011), they wrote, "Carrier personnel have to transform the raw materials of new recruits, fickle technology, and unreliable aircraft into total readiness, just as you have to transform your materials into something that is better than what your competitors have to offer" (p. 36).

Can you hear the alchemy in that statement?

Think about the Tiger Team. They didn't just avoid a disaster, they transformed raw materials into something better, into a creative and timely solution. In fact, the CO_2 cartridge contraption was not the only alchemy that enabled the astronauts to return home. There were others, most notably how the Tiger Team figured out a way to conserve power onboard the ship. In part, these moments of alchemy and innovation occurred because the groups, on the ground and on the ship, interrelated in heedful ways around their challenges and opportunities.

Again in, *Managing the Unexpected*, Weick and Sutcliffe wrote that heedful interrelating "enact[s] alertness, broaden[s] attention, reduce[s] distraction, and forestall[s] misleading simplifications" (p.3). My work and in-the-field research with groups, over almost 30 years, has revealed a similar idea: collective mindfulness (seeing together) increases the possibility of ingenious collaboration. But how can we initiate and sustain this kind of tribal seeing?

Tribal Vision Requires a Certain Mind-Set
Consider this brilliant 2006 bit from Weick and Sutcliffe in their article "Mindfulness and the Quality of Organizational Attention":

Mindfulness, therefore, is as much about the reversal of normalizing as it is about encoding and matching situations with routines. Mindfulness is important because it weakens the tendency to simplify events into familiar events and strengthens the tendency to differentiate events into unfamiliar events. Therefore, less-mindful practice normalizes, more-mindful practice anomalizes. By anomalize we mean that mindfulness captures unique particulars, i.e., differences, nuances, discrepancies, and outliers that slow the speed with which details are normalized. (p. 518)

That statement is genius in what it uncovers about mindfulness and seeing together. It's hard for me to pick a favorite sentence in that paragraph. But here are two of them:

Mindfulness is important because it weakens the tendency to simplify events into familiar events and strengthens the tendency to differentiate events into unfamiliar events. . . . By anomalize we mean that mindfulness captures unique particulars, i.e., differences, nuances, discrepancies, and outliers that slow the speed with which details are normalized.

Weick and Sutcliffe brilliantly reveal why so many tribes don't see well together *and* what can help to correct poor vision. Tribes that don't see well together let the routine of familiar events—and I would add, their familiarity with each other—remove the possibility of seeing anything new or novel. When a tribe tells itself there is nothing new to see, then guess what? There is nothing new to see. When it comes to mindfulness (and seeing together), the belief that there is nothing new to see is a sure way to miss a gorilla standing right in front of you.

If you want to see new potentialities in challenges, opportunities, and your raw materials, your tribe will have to anomalize its everyday events, situations, and views of each other. You do this by breaking a spell that likely has some sway on your tribe. This spell makes tribes lethargic and sometimes even apathetic. Let's call it the *all is normal* spell. The *all is normal* spell convinces a tribe that *today is just like yesterday.*

And *tomorrow will be just like today*. Since everyday events are "normal," the tribe's need for collective seeing is unnecessary. There is no need to notice together, because there's nothing happening that requires it. Everything is just, yep, *normal*. Beyond normalizing events, the *all is normal* spell also takes away a tribe's ability to see each other as individuals with growth potential. Everyone has already been labeled and slotted into what they can and cannot do. Until tribes can see unique elements in their raw materials, as well as in each other, tribal seeing will be limited, to say the least.

If you want to break the *all is normal* spell, here are two anomalizing activities your tribe can practice:

- Value Your Tribe
- Upgrade The Moment

Let's take a look at both.

Value Your Tribe

If a tribe wants to anomalize challenges and opportunities, it first should increase the value and growth potential of each member. The more a tribe values its members and looks for growth potential (for each member), the more likely they are to see challenge and opportunity with fresh eyes. In order to see in new and novel ways, tribes must believe that members can stretch beyond current limits and develop new skills. If a tribe has fixed mind-sets toward each other, they are unlikely to look for new possibilities or ingenious solutions. Why would a tribe waste time looking for new ideas when its members don't believe they have the collective power to realize those ideas? Mindless tribe members have well-trodden views of each other, and those views lead to rigid labels. Mindless tribes assign their members strengths and weaknesses and allow for little movement beyond those assignments.

If you want to anomalize events, start by reconnecting to the unique and increasing value of tribe members.

Try this thought exercise:

Think about a tribe that you are a part of. See your fellow members in your mind's eye. This picture alone is amazing. You all have intersected around space, action, and desire. But it's even more amazing than you think. Consider these three very cool ideas that could increase value and growth.

Very Cool Idea Number 1: *You found each other.*

This is no small feat. Your births coincided close enough to meet and share work. A decade or two farther apart, and the possibility of connection would have been lost to unfortunate timing. Beyond the timing of your births, it's no small feat that, with seven billion options, you found each other. Amazing. Think of the places you've all been and the things you've all done. Are you aware of each other's histories? Do you know what tribe members did prior to their arrival? Do you know their potential for growth?

Very Cool Idea Number Two: *Life choices brought you together.*

Think about the choices you made and circumstances you experienced before you joined your tribe. These zigs and zags have marked your life. Ponder all the places you've lived and decisions you've made that altered your trajectory. Now multiply all of that times the number of people in your tribe. It's staggering to consider what it took to bring you all together. Have you listened to the stories of different tribe members? Do you know the choices that led them to your tribe? Why might these stories matter?

Very Cool Idea Number Three: *The draw, the action, and the desire.* Your shared desire for action and specific changes drew you together like a magnet. You were *drawn, even pulled* to respond. You had a choice, but not really. You believe in this work, whatever *it* is and it draws you all. You hear a call and desire to see a change. This is what makes you a tribe. Do you know why tribe members are passionate about your tribe's mission? What draws different members to the work or the cause?

The Price of Devaluing: Lack of Vision and No Alchemy

I have sat with scores of tribes in trouble. Their faces, conversations, and work were marked by hurt feelings, mounting frustrations, and diminishing hope. In these moments, I've seen tribe members devalue each other. Often they can no longer hide disdain. I've seen, on the faces of tribe members, a desire to yell out, "Out of seven billion options, I'm stuck with you! How incredibly unlucky can I get?" This devaluing mind-set disables collective vision. *If I don't value my tribe members, I won't value their view either.* And when the value of different views weakens, the tribe's ability to see together is restricted or eliminated. Many years ago, in my work, I noticed that tribes that don't value each other also struggled to alchemize. Tribe members that devalue each other are doing more damage than they know. Not only are relational bonds weakened, but, more importantly, the possibility of seeing (and acting) together, which leads to alchemy, is lost in the drama of a tribe gone negative.

Tribes don't have to be full of best friends. In fact, tribe members can and will irritate each other in the process of seeing. But if tribe members consistently devalue each other's views, there is little chance of collective ingenuity. A positive bond and respect enables collective vision. When tribe members have positive feelings toward one another, and value each other, it creates interest to see, to think, and observe together. The mantra of ingenious tribes is "How amazing it is that out of seven billion options, we are together? What will we see and do now that we are together?"

Value the tribe and you take a significant step toward anomalizing events and seeing possibilities.

Upgrade the Moment—Put the Unique Back in the Normal

If the first strategy to *anomalize the everyday* is to increase value for tribe members, then the second is to eliminate the tendency to *devalue everyday moments.* I call this tribal problem *situational degradation.* We have a tendency to lower the importance of certain moments, usually the "ordinary" ones. When moments don't seem all that significant, then it follows that seeing those moments in new ways isn't necessary.

Try another thought exercise.

When it comes to *importance of a moment,* what grade would you give the following moments? The moments in question are on the right side of the table and the grading scale is on the left. Think about each moment and give it a grade based on the definitions.

Type of moment	Grading scale
Building a filter to save the lives of astronauts	A—Really, really important moment with life-altering implications.
Designing a spreadsheet for a project	B—Really important moment with implications.
Staff meetings	C—A "normal" moment with seemingly little to no implications.
Winning the Super Bowl	
Board meetings	D—A moment that's likely right up there with waiting in line to pay for your groceries.
	F—Time wasters.

Take a look at the grades you assigned. Now, think about how your tribe (together) would grade the events (or ones similar to them). The lower your tribe's average—for any of the moments above, or any moment at all—the less likely you are to increase tribal vision. The higher the average, which means there's greater significance assigned, the more likely your tribe would pay attention. Remember what Weick and Sutcliffe wrote about mindfulness? "By anomalize we mean that mindfulness captures unique particulars, i.e., differences, nuances, discrepancies, and outliers that slow the speed with which details are normalized."

When events are "normal" we speed through them and miss possibilities. When we see the unique nature of a moment, we slow down and see differently. What makes us see the uniqueness of a moment? We see the uniqueness of a moment when we increase the value of that moment.

Part of why tribes can't see new potentials, not to mention why they behave badly, is because they devalue their situations (and their work). When tribe members think, *What we're doing doesn't matter or is just another version of yesterday,* they are more likely to miss what is right in front of them. When a tribe views a moment as significant, their vision (and action) is more ingenious *because the significance of the moment compels it.*

Now don't get me wrong. I'm not suggesting that your tribe should treat every moment with the exact same level of intensity. You don't need to play the theme from the movie *Rocky* and fist bump every time you get together. Assigning value to a moment is not about highly extraverted and dramatic behaviors. Those do have a place. But I've seen tribes get all "motivated" and "inspired" and then walk out of the pump-you-up meeting and go right back to sleep. Often the big moment is more about hype. My point is this: if you want to see together what *could be,* you have to stop degrading moments because they seem inconsequential. The more moments matter, the more likely you will care about your collective vision.

Once your tribe has "anomalized" events, and each other, you're ready to see together. In order to see the unique possibilities in your raw materials, first circle and join, then discover.

Ingenious Tribes Circle and Join When Challenges and Opportunities Emerge

First circle—Gather attention around your raw materials
Then join—Direct your best energies and thoughts toward your raw materials

Complex and difficult situations can divide and distract a tribe. Narrow agendas, pet ideas, and unproductive alliances often surface when tribes talk about their challenges and opportunities. These behaviors fracture the goodwill and vision of the tribe. If there is ever a time tribe members should remain unified and simultaneously allow for diversity, it's during strategic *dialogue* (the primary way a tribe sees together). Circling and joining with skill increases the possibility that dialogue will lead to ingenious vision.

What Does It Mean to Circle and Join?

Circling is the decision to gather the tribe's attention around a challenge or opportunity. Joining goes beyond simple attention to add intention—a *collective effort* through observation and conversation. These are related but different actions. Just because you've circled (collective attention), doesn't mean you've joined (collective intention). The *Stanford Encyclopedia of Philosophy* provides helpful definitions of both joint attention and joint intention.

In joint attention, the world is experienced as perceptually available for a plurality of agents. This establishes a basic sense of common ground on which other agents may be encountered as potential cooperators. Shared intention enables the participants to act in that world together intentionally, in a coordinated and cooperative fashion, and to achieve collective goals.

(See http://plato.stanford.edu/entries/collective-intentionality/.)

So we circle to gather attention and we join to direct our better selves (intention) onto one object (in our case a challenge, opportunity, and raw materials).

Start with circling.

Circle

I hinted at the idea of collective attention when I likened your tribe's challenge or opportunity to an autostereogram. Tribes have to circle the "dots" of their challenge or opportunity, because *the creative solution is hidden within.* But simply being in a room together doesn't ensure you're all *present* to the "dots." *A circle is created when a tribe* consciously decides to *be present together* to their challenge or opportunity. What I have noticed in my work is that when a tribe decides to pay attention, to be collectively present, the members' observations and conversations *yield more novel and useful insights.* They *see* better.

I've facilitated many tribal circles where certain members lost connection (presence) to the tribe and the conversation at hand. This was apparent through behaviors such as a change in body posture, vocal tone, or facial expression, a focus on personal technology (texting or emailing), and/or a participation in secondary (side) conversations. That is *not* to say these behaviors always reveal disconnection, but based on the context that developed in these specific interactions, as well as through my verbal confirmation with the "disconnected members," (I asked them if my observation was correct), these behaviors signaled member disconnection. And when they "checked out," the tribe suffered for it. Collective vision diminished.

But that's not the end of the story. At some point, for whatever reason, the mindless members were reenergized by the conversation. Their presence was again *felt* by the tribe. What I have observed in these moments of reconnection is that the entire tribe benefits from the reconnection. What does this mean? *A tribe's ability to see possibilities broadens as their collective attention widens (to include more members).* It seems that paying attention together increases the quality of seeing, which in turn opens the tribe to more potential insights.

Consider this example. We know that paying attention during task performance increases skills for individuals. Dan Siegel, a Harvard-trained psychiatrist and researcher on the brain, in his book *Mindsight* (2009) explores the biological significance of attention. "The brain changes physically in response to experience," he writes, "and new mental skills can be acquired with intentional effort, with focused awareness and concentration" (p. 84).

It seems that when an individual pays attention (mindfulness) while doing an activity, rather than remaining mindless, her brain changes and her skill level (for the activity she's performing) increases. What if the same is true for tribes? Tribes don't have physical brains, but what if their collective ability to *see* increases when they *decide* to be present to the seeing *as they do it? And what if they decide not only to be present, but to bring their best effort and skills to the seeing?* The notion of "bringing our best effort to the seeing" describes the action of *joining*. When tribe members direct their best energies and effort to the seeing, they add to their circling, a deep intention to find the hidden possibilities.

Your tribe would do well to develop some cues or mantras that initiate or reinitiate collective attention. Here are a few possibilities:

- Let's shift to a more mindful conversation.
- Bring your attention to the center (or the circle).
- There's something here for us to pay attention to.
- What do we see?
- What's on our table?

If these don't resonate, develop mantras that trigger and cue mindful circling.

Join

When tribes join, they add their intention to their attention. The word *intention* comes from an old French word that meant to "stretch toward with effort." Joining then means that tribe members stretch toward the challenge or opportunity in the middle of the circle and direct their best collective energy and thinking toward it. The more mindful this joining, the more it can lead to *perceiving what is beneath the surface* and an *imagining of* novel and useful solutions.

How You Enter and Behave in the Circle Matters

I live my life and do my work in the shadow of a simple but powerful principle: *the way you enter a situation has a lot to do with the way it will turn out.* Now, of course there are limits to this idea and sometimes it's just plain wrong. You can enter a situation with a positive attitude and great intentions, and it can still fall apart on you. However, mindsets do influence outcomes. Just head home tonight to your significant other in a foul mood, ready for a fight, and see what happens.

The way your tribe enters a conversation has a lot to do with the outcomes that conversation will yield. The way you direct your collective thinking matters.

When alchemy-producing tribes enter a conversation about a challenge or opportunity, in the midst of the chaos and ambiguity, they direct their intentions toward *insights*. They desire to see the raw materials through different frames and organize those ideas and materials into new possibilities. This begins when tribes *anticipate* insight through their collective vision and conversation.

During times of circling, there are a number of unhealthy alternatives available to tribes. Here are just a few:

- Splintering
- Ambivalence
- Blame
- Distraction

The ambiguity of facing challenges and opportunities can lead to dysfunctional mindsets. In fact, sometimes it may be impossible to avoid them. We can't be at our best in every moment of every conversation. However, dysfunctional strategies that emerge during a conversation are often a cue that a tribe needs to reset the direction of its thoughts. And in what direction do we want the thoughts of the tribe to move during this phase? *Insight.* You join to uncover insights that can lead to the alchemy of your raw materials. *Tribal insight is more likely when it is the explicit desire of the tribe.* Remember the principle above? The way a tribe enters a situation (or conversation) has a lot to do with the way it will turn out. It's likely your tribe knows this principle is important, but it's quite another matter to practice it in the midst of strategic dialogue. Therefore, when your tribe "joins" in the circle, it's important to set "insight" as your intention before you begin. If you're all expecting insight (something we will talk more about later), it is more likely that you will bring your best effort to the circle.

If your tribe is new to directing thoughts toward insight, it's best to begin conversations with that as the stated desire. "Okay, we have X challenge in front of us. We know it's frustrating, but beyond the frustration, there is a creative solution. Let's set our intention toward insight. As we talk, let's do it with an anticipation that something will reveal itself." Now you might think that stating that is just over the top. You might not be able to see your tribe inviting such an intention. Well then, I simply refer you back to the earlier principle stated a bit differently. If you don't think you can do it, you probably can't or won't.

Your tribe would do well to develop some cues or mantras that initiate or reinitiate collective intention. Here are a few possibilities:
- We bring our best energy to this moment
- We stretch toward our challenge/opportunity with intention
- Join the circle (now these words mean something more)

If these don't resonate, develop mantras that trigger and cue mindful circling.

Once you've set your intention, don't force it.

Once your tribe sets insight as its desire, don't work too hard to find the insight during the conversation. Spend your energy on the quality of the conversation about your raw materials and let the insights sneak up on you. If you push too hard for the insight, it will often elude you. If you focus on the raw materials and your tribe's ability to uncover new possibilities, insights will pop. Remember autostereograms? They can be helpful here. I noticed over the years of staring at these pictures that if I tried too hard to find the picture, it didn't reveal itself. I needed a kind of relaxed focus that enabled the picture to pop. Tribes that push too quickly for solutions miss the relaxed but focused nature of the conversations that lead to insight. Set your desire for insight, keep it a part of your tribal psyche during the conversation, and then place your focus on seeing ingenious ways to use what you have. Let the insight come to you.

Smart Tribes Circle and Join Around the Right Stuff

As already mentioned, tribes can easily circle around many things such as personal agendas, jealousies, unproductive frustrations, and a host of other stifling elements. This creates division. But when you join each other in the circle, you are signaling that the challenge or opportunity (the "anomalized" event) and your raw materials are in the center, and for good reason. In other words, what you put in the middle of the circle is as important as the circle itself. And, that's why joining is so critical to circling. It keeps the content of the circle to that which needs alchemy. When you join together, your tribe consciously places the challenge or opportunity (and everything else related) in the middle of the circle. The more you explicitly choose what it is that you are looking at, the greater are your chances of seeing possibilities. Too many meetings or conversations are ineffective because tribe members don't have a common understanding of the topic. They've circled, but not joined around the same issue or idea.

I've witnessed groups swerve so far off topic that the important work of noticing together is buried in talk about lesser things. Sometimes tribes use these conversational diversions as a strategy to avoid the hard work of seeing. It's not easy to keep the challenge or opportunity in the center of the conversation—especially when that conversation is laced with disagreements, frustrations, or obstacles. It's easy to throw lesser items into the center just to ease the tension or get a quick win.

Circling and joining around challenges and opportunities and noticing their contours is hard work.

Here's are some ways to notice if you have lost focus around your raw materials:

Lack of focus: Your conversational meandering isn't taking you into the chaos of the challenge/opportunity, but away from it.

Try this: *If you feel you are inappropriately meandering, rejoin and restate that which should be at the center.*

Lack of focus: You have a challenge or opportunity that keeps showing up on the agenda but never progresses.

Try this: *If you're not making progress, it's time to ask if the main thing has slipped too far off center and if you are no longer joined around it.*

Lack of focus: Your frustration with each other grows unmanageable and you have to table the conversation.

Realize this: *Occasionally this is okay. However, if it's a pattern around a topic, it's likely a stall tactic that eclipses the fact you have lost your ability to join.*

What are some other dysfunctions your tribe uses to keep the main thing off center? How could replace those strategies?

Collective attention as it relates to tribal seeing is the choice to be present together with the raw materials in the center of the circle.

Discover: Once You've Circled and Joined, It's Time to Discover

Words are like potatoes; they are full of rich nutrients (meaning) until we strip them down, deep-fry them, and add salt. The first definition *Merriam-Webster's* provides for the word *discover* is "to see, find, or become aware of (something) for the first time." In a sense, that is accurate, but it's not robust enough. It makes a word that has the nutrients of a potato feel more like a French fry. When we understand more about the meaning of this handy little word, it reveals another important element of seeing together. Break the word in two and it yields its secrets.

Dis: apart, asunder, away
cover: to conceal

The definition of discover, then, is *to throw off that which conceals something else.* Oh, that's good. It's an especially poignant definition for collective seeing. As we now have established, when the raw materials of a situation are in front of your tribe, the possibility or creative solution is initially concealed (hiding in the dots). Discovery then allows your tribe to explore the hidden potential in the raw materials. In order to do this, you have to throw off certain ideas and actions that may be covering up the more novel and useful ones. *Your tribe must throw off that which obfuscates your collective insights.*

Because alchemy requires a new arrangement of familiar materials, this "throwing off" frequently begins when you change your collective view of those materials. No longer are the dots just the same old picture you saw yesterday and the day before that. Now they contain possibilities for alchemy. Now the circle of intentional tribe members can remove obstacles and see new ideas. Here are three actions that enhance the discovery of insights:

- See and listen to different perspectives
- Create a question-to-insight rich environment
- Weave perspectives and ideas together

Let's take a look at each discovery-oriented action. Although it's important to note that *these three elements often occur simultaneously in the discovery process.*

See and Listen to Different Perspectives

For the last seven years, I've had the privilege of teaching a group of young leaders in Arizona the concepts contained in Tribal Alchemy. ALEAD is an organization that works to support the leadership and life development of high school students by providing them with a summer experience that is focused on leadership and law enforcement. Every year, for seven years, I've stood in front of a different group of high school students and explored all manner of alchemy with them. This past year (2015), at one point during the daylong workshop, I talked about the power of taking different perspectives. The students and I talked about how easy it is to view the world form our favorite spot and disregard those who see it differently. We also talked about the dangers that surface when we do this.

During this conversation, I had the students perform a little visual experiment to highlight the reality of different perspectives. One by one, I put a series of pictures up on the screen and asked the students to answer questions about the pictures. For example, one picture depicted a young adult man sitting on a park bench. Sitting next to him was a woman. She had her head on the man's shoulder in what appeared to be a tender moment. Also in the picture, and sitting a foot away (on the same bench), was another woman. This second woman had her arm extended on the bench and was holding the hand of the man behind the back of the first woman. The view of the picture (from the perspective of the beholder) was from the back. The only face of the three that was visible to the beholder was the second woman as she slightly turned to hold the man's hand.

As I put the picture up, I asked the students to write down what each person in the picture was thinking. Here's a sample of what happened next.

Dave: So what's the guy thinking?

Student 1: He's thinking, "I know this is wrong, but I just can't stop."

Student 2: What do you mean? What's he doing that's so wrong?

Student 1: You're kidding, right?

Student 3 to student 2: Who do you think the blonde holding the man's hand is, anyway?

Student 2: It's his wife.

Student 4: His wife?

Student 2: Ya.

Student 1: No, it's his side squeeze. ["Squeeze" was not the word student 1 used, but just go with it.]

Student 2: No way. It's his wife.

Student 4: Okay, let's say it is his wife, then who is the woman leaning up against him?

Student 2: His sister.

At this point, half the room burst out laughing. Some of the students shook their heads in agreement with student 2. Other students looked as if they were now questioning their own view. Others still were quite certain they were right. What seemed like a straightforward view, wasn't so straightforward after all.

It never ceases to amaze me just how many different views can emerge when people "look" at the same thing. When tribal members circle around challenges and opportunities, they see different elements and dynamics. In fact, sometimes they see completely different and even contradictory elements. Mediocre tribes work hard to hurry through their different perspectives in favor of a dominant view. This allows for less ambiguity and quicker resolution. It also significantly diminishes the possibility of alchemy. Ingenious insights don't come as the result of premature agreement. They come out of the squeeze of appropriate tension. That tension comes because people have different views, ideas and possible solutions. This makes lesser tribes exasperated because for them the goal is to achieve control and/or quick resolution. Ingenious tribes embrace the tension, even irritation, that comes from different perspectives. They know that it's the mix of ideas that makes a conversation rich. Further, they know that healthy tension due to different perspectives is exactly what leads to *insight*.

Tribal leaders play a big role in validating this kind of perspective taking. I've watched many leaders shut down a room, not to mention the conversation, because other people "saw it" differently then they did. This "difference" poked at the insecurity of the leader. In an attempt to reassert control, he or she disenfranchised the different ideas and the people who shared them. This ensds the possibility of seeing together, not to mention alchemy. Openhanded leaders, with ego strength, welcome different perspectives because they know it leads to discovery.

If your tribe struggles with perspective taking, try these strategies:

- Be on the lookout for premature agreement. Quick agreement can mean that your tribe's perspective was too limited.
- If your tribe agrees to quickly, assign members to different perspectives. If multiple-perspective taking is not occurring naturally, create it.
- Seek external vision. External eyes may be other tribes inside your community or organization or family. Or it could be voices unrelated in anyway. Outsider voices provide immediate access to differing viewpoints. Outside voices often do not have a full understanding of your tribe's mission or work. It's important to calibrate what they see, but it's also essential that you don't prematurely dismiss it simply because it may lack context.

- Create margin for different perspectives to emerge. When tribe members sense there is little time for differing perspectives, many will simply remain silent. Margin welcomes multiple perspectives.
- Suspend your judgment toward differing perspectives. Differing perspectives won't lead to better tribal vision if they are diminished, disenfranchised, or disrespected. Dialogue requires that we hold loosely our own opinions about differing views. Subtle and sometimes not so subtle bad attitudes, body postures and facial expressions diminish different perspectives and make it impossible for a free exchange of ideas to occur.

Find the nuggets in different views and put them together.

Create A Question-To-Insight Rich Environment

Our experience suggests that human systems grow and construct their future realities in the direction of what they most persistently, actively, and collectively ask questions about.

James D. Ludema, Benedictine University

David L. Cooperrider, Case Western Reserve University Frank

J. Barrett, Naval Postgraduate School

...

Most tribes know that an environment conducive to question-making is required for discovering insight. Some tribes though, in the messiness of the conversation, ignore questions in favor of declarations. Other tribes just don't have a strategy in place that helps them remember to ask questions. And others have a strategy for question-making but just don't use it at critical moments in the dialogue. However, when tribes remember to create questions of discovery, they increase the possibility of insight. The good news is that tribes can create the environment where questions are more likely. And that can lead to insights necessary for ingenuity. Let's consider then how to create a *question-to-insight-rich environment.*

Creating a question-to-insight rich environment

I've always been a fan of the word "intercourse." We usually reserve the word *intercourse* for sex. In fact, if you don't modify the word *intercourse* with another word, like *social*, the foregone conclusion is that you're referring to physical sex. This is a tad unfortunate, because the word "intercourse" (including the sexual act) brilliantly describes what is needed to create *a question-to-insight-rich environment*. So let's think about intercourse, including the physical kind, as a model for creating a *question-to-insight-rich* environment.

What Do We Want? Tribes that conceive insights through the fertilization of ingenious questions

Alchemy-producing tribes are looking to conceive insights that can lead to alchemy. This conception happens when ingenious *questions fertilize a discovery-oriented tribe.* The moment of tribal insight (aha) is the *moment of conception* that can lead to alchemy. Therefore, when timely and well crafted questions meet a tribe with an open mindset, those questions fertilize the tribe with the seed of possibility. In other words, the tribe gets pregnant with a robust insight. That's what we want. But how do we get that? Well let's keep pushing the metaphor.

First, create space

Question-to-insight-rich environments require tribes to make space. This is why circling and joining are essential to seeing and discovering. You have to have a space for the "conceiving" to occur. Once again, the current and unfortunate view of "meetings" diminishes the value of *space to question and conceive.* There is general drudgery associated with meetings because so many are boring and *unproductive* (they don't conceive anything). Generative spaces (where tribes meet to explore) are places where conception occurs and tribes should view it that way. Effective tribes want to get pregnant with great ideas through conversation and question making, because that's how *it* happens. So...they make the space to question and think together.

Then, wonder out loud

Okay, stay with me now. Lots of sperm work to be "the one" to fertilize a physical egg. So it takes a lot of wondering together to fertilize a tribe's ability to discover insights. You have to generate a lot of questions and ideas to get to the ones that lead to insight. Questions fuel wondering because they push tribes to get ideas out and explore them. There will be a lot of ideas that don't make it to the aha moment. That's okay. The ideas that don't make it often lead to the ones that do. Conversational wondering is about many ideas that lead toward rather than away from insight. The ideas that don't make it shouldn't be viewed as a waste but as necessary iterations that make insight possible.

In order to wonder, tribes will have to embrace intelligent ignorance (a precondition of question-making). Smart discussion requires that we bring our best intelligence and wisdom without letting either of those elements lead us to believe we have nothing new to learn or appreciate. In order to do this, make sure you monitor how much time passes between meaningful questions.

If you're not asking enough questions along the way, your conversation won't lead to insight. Tribes should monitor how often questions are asked and if those questions are generative. If you're stuck at any given moment in a conversation of discovery, try this practice: *ask three more questions.* Sometimes you have to prime the pump with a series of questions before the right one emerges. The "three more questions" practice shifts tribes into the mind-set of wondering.

If you're really stuck you could ask these questions:

- If we had to turn this part of the conversation into a question, what would that question be?
- What questions are we afraid to ask?
- Is it possible we are avoiding questions?
- What type of questions have helped us in the past?

Next (you're going to love this one) pay attention to tribal ovulation

There are certain moments where, during questions and conversations of discovery, it all comes together for a tribe and the great idea is about to emerge. Tribes need to learn to read when these moments are close and stay with it. But, when you know you're close to insight, increase engagement for question-making and discovery based conversations. We will discuss this more in process step three (engage it). Also, when the great idea emerges, get it down so you don't forget it. Creating an identity for an insight is part of process step two (name it).

Finally, Make Sure Your Questions are Potent—The Danger of Pseudo Question-Making

We can't leave this idea without recognizing and exploring pseudo-questions. It is possible for tribe members to ask questions that aren't really questions. This diminishes the *question-to-insight* environment and the possibility of alchemy.

Pseudo questions are clever ways to get our points across without being overly directive. Sometimes we do this because we want to beat around the bush, and sometimes we do it in order to appear curious when we're already locked in to a view point.

Here are some examples of pseudo question making:

- The, *I'm going to phrase my question in a way that forces you to agree with me* question
- The, *I found a clever way to put a question mark on a statement* question
- The, *I have an agenda that I'm trying to disguise as a question* question
- The, *I think your idea is terrible and I'm going to discount it with a question* question
- The, *I'm deflated and I want you to be deflated too so I'm going to ask a sarcastic question* question

Pseudo questions have the potential to shut tribal vision down because they call into question the motives of the question-maker. It takes a measure of trust, transparency and even vulnerability to create conversational intercourse. Pseudo questions add an element of deception to the conversation that derails it. If you have something to say, say it. Don't dress it up in a fancy question. If you have something to say, but you also want to frame it as a question, then be transparent about that. "Okay, I'm really struggling to see the value of this opportunity. It seems to me that we will distract ourselves if we pursue it. So, with that in mind, can we talk about the potential dangers of this opportunity and how we keep it from derailing progress?"

Pseudo questions have a particular goal: *I want to tell you something but I'm going to, for whatever the reason, phrase my statement like a question.*

If conception is your aim, then the way you frame your questions and deliver them, matters.

Weave Perspectives and Ideas Together

As we've seen, multiple perspectives enable tribes to generate varied and robust ideas. When it comes to tribal vision, idea-generation gives a tribe the initial "stuff for the conversation." Idea generation is important because it becomes part of a tribe's raw materials. However, idea generation alone is not enough to lead a tribe to insight. We need to add another dynamic to idea generation. I call this next action *idea weaving*. Idea weaving occurs when pieces of perspectives are retrieved from the conversation and layered together in order to make a more robust collective idea. It's the collective idea, this superidea, that provides a tribe with the possibility of alchemy.

The alchemy of ideas leads to the alchemy of action.

Integrate the best of the different perspectives

Discovery is less likely if your tribe approaches idea-exploration with a "king of the hill" mentality. The best ideas are rarely singular, that is, coming from one person or one view. Rather, the moment of insight is the result of multiple ideas and perspectives at play in conversational intercourse. Idea weaving, to use a different metaphor, occurs when tribe members *explore and evaluate combinations of ideas*, then *keep track of those ideas as the conversation widens*, and finally *integrate the ideas with "chemistry."*

Explore and evaluate combinations of ideas

We know that if a tribe wants to conceive insights it has to have the space explore questions and ideas. In order to evoke and explore ideas, however, it takes more than space. Creating a circle and joining with intent is critical, but it's not enough. As ideas emerge, tribes have to find a way to hold, explore, and experiment with various combinations of ideas. Doing so enables better tribal vision and the likelihood of alchemy. Holding, exploring, and experimenting with combinations of ideas is kind of like taking ideas on a date. You want to see if there's any chemistry between them. Ideas in isolation won't create the serendipitous aha moment needed for tribal seeing or alchemy.

Ideas gain power as they bond to other ideas throughout the conversational process. This bonding process requires tribe members to engage in both divergent and convergent thinking. If tribes want to weave ideas together into creative solutions, they must shift back and forth between these two types of thinking. Much of what I've described as important to tribal seeing is related to divergent thinking. Divergent thinking occurs when tribes pursue multiple perspectives, ideas, and questions. There is not one right idea but rather an openness to multiple ideas and, more importantly, multiple questions. This divergent approach is essential to idea weaving. However, convergent thinking is also important to idea weaving.

Arthur Cropley, retired professor from the University of Hamburg, spent his life studying creativity. In his 2006 article "In Praise of

Convergent Thinking," which appeared in the *Creativity Research Journal,* he described convergent thinking this way:

> Convergent thinking is oriented toward deriving the single best (or correct) answer to a clearly defined question. It emphasizes speed, accuracy, logic, and the like and focuses on recognizing the familiar, reapplying set techniques, and accumulating information. (p. 391)

In the same article, Cropley goes on to describe the interplay between convergent and divergent thinking:

> I do not intend to deny the importance of divergent thinking in production of effective novelty. However, although necessary, it is not sufficient on its own except perhaps for occasional flukes when blind luck leads to effective novelty. Convergent thinking is necessary, too, because it makes it possible to explore, evaluate, or criticize variability and I identify its effective aspects. In the enthusiasm for divergent thinking, it is thus important not to forget the contribution of convergent thinking, although it is also important not to overemphasize it as I believe is usually done in schools and universities. (p. 398)

This powerful insight reveals that idea weaving occurs when tribes evoke and explore (divergent) as well as analyze and evaluate (convergent) ideas. These two types of conversational thought processes are the weaving tools of a tribe. If you don't have both tools, your weave is going to lack either novelty (not enough divergent thinking) or usefulness (not enough convergent thinking). There is a back-and-forth motion between these types of thinking that enables ideas to become interwoven with wisdom (making them more likely to be both novel and usable).

Weaving ideas together that work won't occur unless those ideas are analyzed, criticized, and tested by the current context of the tribe. Great ideas remain just that if they cannot be manifested in the concrete world. If a tribe doesn't add convergent thinking to divergence, it is possible that the results may not create the needed change. Overemphasis of divergence, in the name of creativity, can lead to all sorts of unintended consequences. Tribes must be careful in their free thinking not to associate boundaries and limitations as the enemy. For instance, in brainstorming the "no bad idea" rule is just wrong. Some ideas are unsubstantiated and untested and should not be irresponsibly entertained in the name of "getting out of the box." The opposite outcome is also possible. Some divergent ideas are dismissed by a tribe—without any consideration or analysis—because they are too far "out there." At that point, reactivity rather than evaluation frames the rejection, and great ideas are lost for good.

The trick is to learn to switch, at the right time, from divergent to convergent and from convergent to divergent thinking. If you switch too fast or too often, you may not give the current thought process its due. However, if you switch too slow, you encounter dysfunctions in tribal seeing. If you switch too slow out of divergent thinking, you are susceptible to an idea fest that never leads to actionable alchemy. If you switch too slow out of convergent thinking, you are susceptible to idea stagnation that limits the options for alchemy. This ability to switch at the right times and in the right ways is a skill of great importance and value. Tribes would do well to discuss which type of thinking they favor and how to switch between them with greater skill. Wise facilitation is also valuable as a tribe learns to switch or is facing a more difficulty set of conversations.

Keep track of ideas as the conversation widens

Another part of idea weaving has to do with holding and keeping ideas. During idea generation and weaving, tribe members must keep a number of ideas in play. The trick is to hold onto ideas so that you don't lose them while simultaneously exploring certain ideas more deeply than others. When an idea surfaces in a conversation, it may not be time to explore it. However, that doesn't mean the idea that surfaced is not useful. Many times "out of place" ideas are later inserted (at just the right moment) to fill in a piece of the weaving. Because of this, don't discard ideas too quickly. You need a holding mechanism that allows your tribe to return to ideas when the time is right. Many tribes use some kind of idea-capturing process that allows them to see multiple ideas at once. Some use white boards, others use small sticky notes, still others use more technologically savvy options.

No matter what capturing tool you use, what's critical is that you find a way to return to an idea when it makes sense in the flow of the conversation. Your chosen tool will help you with this piece of the process, but it's not a silver bullet. It's up to tribe members to bring ideas back at the right time. This is often a serendipitous moment because the newly inserted idea leads to great insight. This is why the "king of the hill" mentality just won't do. If everyone in the conversation is trying to protect his or her idea and minimize the value of other ideas, it will be far less likely that ideas are integrated. This is the end of great conversation.

In tribal conversations and in tribal seeing, it is the collective effort that brings the best ideas into the circle. When tribe members are too concerned about individual ownership of ideas, it lessens the possibility of tribal vision. Don't get me wrong—I'm all for individual contribution. I'm all for giving credit to ideas when they come from a single author. However, if we've learned anything in the last 200 years, it's that great ideas are never born in isolation. Great innovations and inventions are tribal, even if that tribe contains a dominant voice. Thomas Edison is credited with the invention of the light bulb. Yet we know that many other people worked alongside him. Without these other voices, his genius might have been lost. Scientists know that sharing information is the pathway to break through. Hoarding information is the pathway to puny ideas and anemic solutions that are often unsustainable or just wrong.

Idea weaving requires tribes to unselfishly hold ideas, integrate them at the right time, and welcome joint effort as much as individual contribution.

Integrate the ideas with chemistry

Idea weaving is the result of capturing ideas, holding them loosely, and inserting them at the right moment. Once your tribe has an idea of substance, you will notice that idea takes on an identity. It starts to take shape and has texture. It becomes more than an idea; it becomes a possible future. This is a very tenuous moment for a collective idea. It is not yet alchemy, but it is more than a speculation. At this point, it's important to foster the identity of the idea. This fostering of an idea takes us to the second step in the process of Tribal Alchemy. When ideas are born, it's important to name them. That second step gives the idea identity, and it gives the tribe the ability to return to the idea no longer as random or disconnected thoughts but as a growing possibility that could lead to alchemy.

Tying it all together

We've explored a lot of ground—not to mention a number of metaphors in this section. But just remember this: Seeing together is about conceiving insights that can lead to alchemy. The way your tribe comes together (circles), directs energy and effort (joins) and discovers possible insights through an open to question environment makes the difference in what you will see—and therefore in what you will create.

NAME

Doctor: It's a girl.

Nurse: Oh, how sweet. What are you going to name her?

Dad: Name her?

Nurse: Yes, what name did you choose for your daughter?

Mom: Oh, we've decided not to name her.

Awkward silence and stares in the room

Nurse (trying to relieve the moment): You mean you're going to name her when you get home?

Dad: Nah, we don't plan on it. She's going to just be our nameless bundle of joy.

When I teach on the importance of "naming," I always ask for a show of hands to see how many parents are in the room. Once I have the hands of the parents in the air, I ask another question: "How many of you named your kids?" The audience normally laughs because of obvious irony. Parents name children, end of discussion. Not only that, but they often labor for months over just the right name. To do less than that would be to shirk responsibility. In fact, in many nations, there are laws that require a name to be given to a child before she or he leaves the hospital. Even if the law isn't explicit, the expectation is. Nations also have laws that place boundaries on what names can be used. In 2007, the BBC reported about one "name rebel" couple that protested the "naming laws" of Sweden by submitting this name:

Brfxxccxxmnpccccclllmmnprxvclmnckssqlbb11116

It was rejected, if you can imagine that.

All of this shows just how seriously we humans take the naming of children. In many cultures, names are given as a defining hope for a child's life. But of course, our penchant for naming doesn't stop with children. Humans name, well, just about everything. Think about it; to "name" just a few:

- People
- Projects
- Storms
- Buildings
- Initiatives
- Schools
- Art
- Hospitals
- Accomplishments
- Trees
- Plants
- Animals
- Instruments
- Food

In his essay "How to Name Things," writer and founder of the blog *ribbonfarm*, Venkatesh Rao wrote in 2012, "We name to liberate, and we name to imprison. We name to flatter, and we name to insult. We name to own, and we name to be owned. We name to subsume, and have subsumed. We name to frame, and we name to reframe."

As Rao points out, names define and describe in ways that can be positive or negative. I use the concept of naming as a positive and essential part of Tribal Alchemy. Through naming, we bring challenges and opportunities into focus, give them texture and shape, as well as provide ourselves with a way to behave in the midst of them. It is also possible to see a name as a stifling designation that limits and controls. However, for that idea, I use the word "label."

Naming Creates Identity

Ironically, of all the things we name, challenges and opportunities sometimes remain unnamed for too long. Naming a challenge or opportunity provides it with an identity. Creating that identity is critical to alchemy. Ideas in need of alchemy are often ambiguous and difficult to manifest. Turning ideas into action is a challenge for the most seasoned of tribes (and their leaders). The ability to find the magic in the mess is the holy grail of human endeavors. Naming can be a helpful step in giving shape to the mess and enabling your tribe to understand and to describe the dynamics related to it.

Names describe. When we name challenges and opportunities, the name supplies the tribe with analogies, metaphors, and other ideas that bring them to life, or at least into focus. Naming enables a tribe to circle and join around a real obstacle or possibility and conceive of more meaningful and igneous solutions. It also creates an identity that shapes the tribes and the anticipated alchemy. Cherryl Armstrong and Sheryl Fontaine, in their article "The Power of Naming: Names that Create and Define the Discipline," wrote, "By naming something, one actively carves out a space for it to occupy, a space defined by what one values in the phenomenon and by how it appears to be like or unlike other parts of one's world view. James Britton explains that by conferring names on objects, we engage in a 'process of bringing into existence the objects of the immediate environment'" (p. 7–8).

Can you hear the beginnings of alchemy in these words? Because names create identity, which, as Fontaine and Armstrong explain, "carves out a space for that 'named something' to occupy." This is exactly what a tribe does when it names what it sees in its circle.

. . .

I recall working with a tribe of social entrepreneurs who were focused on the implementation of a new strategic initiative. This initiative was mission-critical, and the outcomes were directly related to their future success. Much of the tribe's community credibility was riding on the success of the initiative. The initiative required that the tribe partner with several external stakeholders. These stakeholders had community capital, and the primary tribe needed their support. Early on in the work, a few of the external stakeholders resisted the goals of the initiative as well as various tribe members. These external stakeholders struggled to understand the initiative and its purpose. They directly challenged the validity of the work and expressed increasingly strong feelings of disapproval in joint meetings. You could feel the pressure rise and the initiative stall.

After a couple of difficult meetings, I suggested the primary tribe "name" the challenge. "What name could represent what's going on right now?" I asked. "How would you sum it up?"

"Stuck in the mud," was spontaneously offered. I often find that when asked a straightforward question about the challenge or opportunity, the spontaneous answer provides important insights. After "stuck in the mud" was blurted, we all laughed and agreed that indeed that was the general state of things. For reasons I'll soon explain, I suggested the initial name "stuck in the mud" needed refinement. The tribe ended up naming the challenge "getting out of the mud." Immediately after the name was chosen, the conversation was infused with greater clarity about the problems and potential solutions associated with the challenge. Tribal energy increased as the tribe created a strategic action plan that was sensitive to those involved.

Naming the tribal challenge created value and gave the frustration an identity. The name made the situation more real. It was almost as if the challenge now had a seat at the table, a place to occupy, that allowed the tribe to more effectively engage it. Before the name, the obstacle and the desired change were diffuse and ambiguous. After the name, it was a "living project" that had boundaries and descriptions and needed a certain kind of attention from the tribe.

It's not necessarily a difficult task to give a challenge or opportunity an initial name. Tribes spend a lot of time talking about both challenge and opportunity, so there is ample time to name them. What is needed is a shift in the conversation that moves it from an examination of disparate parts to a summarization of parts into a flexible whole.

The name is not meant to trivialize or minimize the complexity of the issues, but rather to create a metaphor for both the current situation and the desired future state.

Naming Creates Commitment and Ownership

When I hear the names Matthew and Andrew, they evoke something deep within me. Barbara, Mary, Sam, and Paul are also fine names. But they just don't do it for me. I don't have the same connection to those names. Matthew and Andrew are the names of my two adult sons. When I ponder those names, I think of the years of investment, delight, and, yes, struggle that have marked my relationship with them. As I open up my memory and imagination, I can hear myself calling their names as they arrived home from the hospital, took their first steps, managed the complexities of school, discovered the joys and frustrations of the world, perplexed me with their decisions, delighted me with their insights, and reminded me of my love for them. I'm committed to them in a different, singular, and ongoing way. I don't own them, of course. But I do own a responsibility to them that has shaped my life for over 27 years.

. . .

Naming challenges and opportunities creates commitment and ownership. When tribe members perpetually complain about a challenge or an opportunity, the language is specific but not focused. They talk about the particulars of the situation, but there is no overall focus that brings it to life. But when a challenge or opportunity is named, it can no longer remain diffuse. The carved-out space now requires the tribe to do something with it. Ownership and commitment are essential for alchemy because they energize the tribe with desire for change. Just as the names Matt and Drew move me to action, so do tribal names in creating a compelling reason (and path) for action.

Consider a tribe of professionals I coached. Many of them had fallen into a snare of bad attitudes. Eye rolls, deep sighs, painful emotions and sarcastic comments peppered the conversations during most shifts. They were a courageous group of experts who were deeply committed to their work, but frustrated by what they viewed as external issues around them.

When we met, I listened to the stories that were told and the frustrations expressed. I knew that, along with supporting them, I would have to challenge them if I was going to help them alchemize their world. I can still remember the moment of challenge when I stretched them beyond their comfort zone. As we sat together, I shared that I believed they had three choices before them. It was time to make a conscious choice of one of the options. I named each choice simply door number one, two, and three. I chose the "door metaphor" because it signified an action that, if chosen, would situate the "chooser" into a very specific set of attitudes and actions. Here were the three choices connected to the three doors:

Door number one: Stay in the system and just keep complaining and vomiting frustration.

Door number two: Stay in the system and become a tribe of alchemists who see the realistic challenges and turn them into something better—even with limitations.

Door number three: Look for different jobs.

We considered together what each door would mean if they chose it. "Sometimes door number three is a valid door to open," I explained. I told a story of my own need to move on from a career and job that had defined me in a direction I no longer embraced. Though my goal was not to persuade any of them to leave, I wanted to have an honest rather than "threat-based" conversation about the possibility of leaving the organization. Door number one, I explained, was also an option. But I asked the tribe to consider what value it held for them individually and collectively. "Do you really want to hit yourselves over the head with a hammer?" I noted that perpetual complaining would lead them to self-inflicted wounds—wounds they would feel more deeply than anyone else in the organization. Perpetual complaining eventually hurts the complainer in ways he or she is not expecting or desiring. "Is the potential backfire worth the risk?" I asked.

I then talked about door number two and the reason I believed it was the best option for those who were going to stay. We discussed why alchemy was the better choice and I gave them opportunity to agree or disagree with this assumption. "If you're staying, choose door number two," I implored. "Door number two will not only reenergize you as tribe members, but it will increase your ability to create ingenious solutions to the very problems you're currently complaining about. If you want to see change, and your choice is to stay, door number two is a better ride and, more importantly, the way to create alchemy."

We spent a good hour discussing the consequences, the frustrations, and the implications of each door. Some of the conversation was difficult and some of it lighthearted. But the naming of the three choices (door number one, two, and three) made each one more real. They took on identity, and, more importantly, they became more tangible choices. Now the tribe members would have to "own" their door. This was a critical shift that needed to occur. Up to this point, bad attitudes were acceptable because tribe members believed their bad attitudes weren't chosen but rather inflicted on them by external situations. Now the names placed personal choice at the center of each member's behavior.

Tribe members would have to own their behavior rather than excuse it due to the dysfunctions of others. The tribe members seemed energized, though somewhat apprehensive, by this newfound commitment and responsibility.

After the meeting, I received feedback that the phrase "door number two" had gone viral among the tribe—even among those who had not been at the initial meeting. The phrase became an icon for a change of attitude and behavior. It became a marker of commitment and ownership. Tribe members shared the "door conversation" with other members who had not been at the original meeting. I was asked to come talk to other tribe members and "give the door speech." Tribe members asked each other what "door they had chosen." The name created ownership for the tribe. But it also created commitment. In a way, it took away all the diffuse talk and attitude, as well as the ability to avoid responsibility. After the door conversations, if a tribe member engaged in unproductive complaining, he or she was choosing a door with implications. The names also became the way tribe members held each other accountable. When complaining broke out, people challenged each other by saying, "door number two." That phrase reestablished commitment and ownership to a better path.

What's important in this example is not just how the name changed the dynamics of tribe members toward each other. What's important is that the name refocused tribe members on alchemy. Remember, Tribal Alchemy isn't about "team building." Tribal Alchemy is about the discovery of creative solutions that come as the result of seeing and using your raw materials in ingenious ways. "Door number two" was about more than the transformation of attitudes. It was about a refocus on the tribe's shared outcomes. That's what names do: they create a focus on change, and they rally the attention of the tribe to make that change more likely.

How to Name Challenges and Opportunities: Choose the Name and the Frame Wisely

As we've discovered, when it comes to your raw materials, the view of your tribe matters. Perception influences behavior in powerful ways. Each tribe member brings his or her own view to a situation. Those perceptions then comingle to create a dominant tribal view. This is how a tribe's "frame"—around just about anything—is formed. Small interactions and conversations lead to a dominant view, which then influences the behavior of the tribe. Soon, those behaviors habituate in norms. Norms determine then what is and is not acceptable thinking and action as a tribe moves forward and as it integrates new members. These perceptual frames become *transparent influencers* of the tribe and often hold back the possibility of change. But these influencers begin through the words and names tribes associate to their situations.

Think about the frames created from this language:

- This place is so screwed up.
- Wait till I tell you what the our *genius leader* has come up with now.
- Well, once again our request was denied.
- People here just don't get it, and we always pay for it.
- I'm sick of being the one to clean up the mess.

When words like those above dominate the conversation of a tribe, the frames that emerge are dysfunctional and unproductive. This is why the process of mindfully naming is so critical to alchemy. Naming can initiate or alter a tribal frame in both positive and negative (labeling) ways. It also shapes the mind-set of the tribe in a similar fashion. You don't name a challenge or opportunity just so you can identify or even commit to it. You name it because the words you choose represent a better way to perceive the emerging situation. As the better perception takes hold, new and more strategic mind-sets and actions will follow. This may take some time, but better names and frames will reshape difficult situations as well as tribal perspectives.

Remember the tribe that was stuck in the mud? What if they had named that challenge "frustrated in the mud." Or "resistance in the mud." Or "Help! I've fallen and I can't get out of the mud." The problem with those names is the defeating nature of the frame. Though each name reveals *a part* of the situation, they are all missing a second important element: *the desired future state.* By naming the challenge "getting out of the mud," the tribe quickly achieved a name that met both criteria for a good frame. What are those two criteria? Names, and frames they help to create, must be both realistic *and* optimistic.

Realistic Names

Realistic names reveal the harder realities of the challenge or opportunity. Realistic names and frames remind the tribe that overcoming obstacles and seizing possibilities takes hard work and requires discipline, courage, and grit. If a name or frame is not realistic, people lose faith in the process and (often) their leaders. Why is this? If the name/frame is rose colored, the incongruence between that name and the reality of the circumstances can cause skepticism, deflation, and even sarcasm. If tribal members or leaders understate the challenge in an attempt to keep morale up, energy for alchemy wanes before the tribe even begins. Creating frames and language that understates the difficulty is an easy but unwise strategy. This is why the group I worked with chose "out of the mud." It was a realistic name in that it focused on their current state of being stuck.

Challenge is part of forward movement. Opportunity too is laced with hard work and setbacks. Smart tribes honor and accept these realities. When a tribe diminishes the hard places, it can fill some members with false hope, which leads to long-term disappointment. Diminishment of difficulty can lead other members to a disbelief in the future due to the unrealistic ideas of the tribe and its leaders. Energy wanes. Because both false hope and disbelief lead to less alchemy, when a tribe faces difficulty they should *own it*. This begins with the language they use to describe it. This doesn't mean leaders or tribe members have to share every gory detail of trouble. But they do need to speak with candor about the issues ahead. The tribe deserves such honesty and should be given the opportunity to rise to the occasion.

It would have been easy to tell the struggling "door number one, two and three professionals" that everything would be okay. I could have told them to just hang in there and wait for things to get better. The problem with such advice is that it lacks realism. "Hanging in there" can make things worse. Things get better through the hard work of alchemy. In an attempt to ease the blow, tribal leaders and members may create false-positive descriptions of genuinely tough situations. This creates more trouble—trouble that is hard to overcome because it leaves tribe members unsure if and how to commit to the work ahead. When you name your challenges and opportunities, be real.

Be Optimistic

Optimism adds actionable hope to the name. *Optimism is not just a desire for change, but a willingness to work toward a creative solution—with hope attached.* That future state is in some way better than the current state and worth the work. Optimism is not the opposite of realism. Optimism can, and must, exist alongside realism. If a name/frame is realistic, but not optimistic, apathy and lethargy aren't far behind. When I shared with the professionals the three door options, I didn't tell them that any old choice would do just fine. I inspired them to make the best choice possible, whatever that might have been for them. One thing is for sure, the choice to stay and perpetually whine and complain was not encouraged. In fact, I shared why that door would eventually lead to a demise. I also didn't encourage anyone to leave the organization, although that is sometimes a very optimistic thing to do. I couldn't make that determination for them. However, I did tell the tribe that leaving was better than staying and vomiting poison into the stream of the organization. I have witnessed far too many people who stay in tribes based on the "hang in there" advice. In doing so, they have done significant damage to themselves and others.

What I encouraged the majority of the tribe to do was choose to stay and alchemize. I spoke to them in inspiring tones—challenging them to be the change and the solution to their complaints. I painted a picture of what they could become and the hard work it would take to get there. In the midst of a difficult conversation, there was laughter, some tears, some pain, but also there was energy to advance. This was, of course, just one conversation led by an outsider (me). The key, as I told them, was to sustain such realism and optimism over a long period of time.

Names that reflect both optimism and realism set the tribe in a favorable space for change. They also ignite energy for that change that leads us to the third step in our process. Before we get to the third step, let's consider a few naming strategies that can help your tribe create great names.

Shifting Conversations in Order to Name

Sometimes naming happens quite naturally. The conversation easily leads a tribe to a word or phrase that sticks. When this happens, the tribe needs to quickly seize the name. Sometimes, though, naming takes some work and requires a bit of collective thought. When considering names for challenges and opportunities, here are a few strategies to keep in mind.

Snippets into a Whole

Because tribes spend a lot of time talking about both challenge and opportunity, what is needed is a way to shift a conversation from an examination of disparate parts to a flexible view of the whole. This shift is not meant to trivialize or minimize the complexity of the issues, but rather to create a global metaphor or descriptor for both the current situation and the desired future state. The question then is, how do you make this shift and move from the parts to a meaningful whole?

During tribal conversations it is possible to simply ask, "If you had to name this challenge or opportunity, what name would you give it?" Sometimes that question is enough to get a tribe thinking creatively about the name. However, sometimes that question misses the mark because tribe members may not be able to switch into a more creative "naming space," particularly if they are in the midst of a difficult conversation. In order to get the naming juices flowing, the tribe can lay out pieces of the conversation and consider what those pieces reveal to the tribe. It's almost as if you are cutting out pictures as you talk and then putting those pictures together like a collage. The snippets of the conversation become a collage, and that picture reveals the name. Take the "getting out of the mud" conversation. It included the following fragments:

- We're stuck.
- Our external stakeholders are resisting.
- This initiative is causing some people angst.
- Moving stakeholders forward is critical to our credibility.
- Pushing stakeholders too quickly could be detrimental.
- We are not moving.

All of these elements came together to form "getting out of the mud." The word "getting" signified that time and process would be involved in reaching the desired state. Though the tribe wanted to hurry people out of the mud, they knew that rushing people could cause them to resist even more. This would require a wise speed—not too slow, which would perpetuate stuck-ness, but not too fast, which could cause unnecessary angst. The phrase "out of the mud" signified the stuck nature of the struggle and that the process was likely to be a bit messy. If you've ever been stuck in thick mud, you know it's messy and also restricts movement in awkward ways. You slip and slide, and mud gets caked on clothes, shoes, and body parts. This visual gave the tribe a way to appreciate the work ahead and what would be required to bring about their desired future state. Many little snippets of the conversation led to one big metaphor that made the difference.

When your tribe is gathering snippets to form a name, ask these questions:

- What do these segments tell us when we put them together?
- What's the common message contained in the snippets?
- If this challenge or opportunity were a picture, what would it be?

Here are other questions to help your tribe think about the qualities of your challenge or opportunity and names that might fit:

- If our current challenge/opportunity were an object, what would it be?
- If our current challenge/opportunity were a TV show, what show would it be?
- If our current challenge/opportunity were an animal, what animal would it be?

Why are these types of questions important? The three questions above, and others like them, allow the tribe to think globally about the challenge and/or opportunity. They also provide a bridge to a name. Once your tribe is thinking globally, it's easier to name the challenge/opportunity. As the tribe thinks about these, or other kinds of questions, they will offer up names. It is often in this exchange that the right combination is found and the tribe finds agreement.

The Serendipitous Home Run Phrase

Occasionally when a tribe is circled around a challenge/opportunity, someone makes a home-run comment that so beautifully sums up the global view that it should become the name. A few years ago I worked with a tribe that had a poor external image with its customers. They worked hard and within difficult limitations. They also believed they were doing good by their customers. But some of their influential customers did not agree. I was asked to come in and spend some time with them.

Initially, the tribe felt they were being unfairly targeted. Some of my early meetings were spent helping them accept the view of customers, whether they agreed with it or not. They knew they had to shift perception as much as possible—to go above what was required. We also acknowledged that some customers were just grumpy, but that would not be a reason to give up on creating fans. The tribe decided that grumpy customers would not be a convenient excuse for mediocre work.

After some time in the conversation, I asked the tribe to name this challenge/opportunity. Initial ideas were bandied about, but none resonated. I threw out an idea. "You know, it feels to me you want to change the view of your customer. What about 'change their view'?" A few people shook their heads, but still no resonance. Then a tribe member said, "Actually, it's not their view that needs to change, it's ours. We need to change OUR view." The whole room immediately agreed and the name, and frame, was born.

When these moments of resonance around a name occur, tribes need to seize them. When there is unanimous resonance around a name or frame, there should be a reverence toward that moment. Collective agreement and energy of this sort is powerful and should be respected. These moments mark critical insights and stimulate collective action.

Naming is a powerful step in the alchemy process because it carves out a place for your challenge or opportunity. It creates identity and ownership, as well as a frame of perception that is realistic and optimistic. When all this occurs, it increases energy for the work and for alchemy. Over and over, in a variety of different settings, I've observed the process of naming ignite a tribe with energy and inspiration for the work ahead. This kind of engagement leads us right to the third step in our process.

ENGAGE

I'm In

We sat on plastic chairs that were both ugly and uncomfortable. Prior to the meeting, there was silence in the room—that is, other than the occasional squeak of a chair that signaled the discomfort of a group member. I knew no one in the room. I was in the room because I had been asked to "help a team in trouble." It's always fun to be called into such a situation because disaster looms like heavy clouds before a downpour.

As the meeting started, I had the feeling there had already been a premeeting. There seemed to be a pact between members. Keep your head down and don't engage. Since this wasn't my first rodeo, I too had a premeeting with myself. I had already thought about what I would do if the group seemed apathetic and lethargic.

We made it through the pleasantries of "hello." Then I asked my first question, which destabilized the pact.

Dave: "Do you want to be here?"

Every head turned up and looked at me like I had just asked, "Do you enjoy trips to the dentist?"

Dave: "No, seriously, do you want to be here?"

Group member: "Isn't the answer obvious?"

Dave: "What answer?"

Member: "The answer is we have no idea why we are here" (some heads shook in the affirmative).

Dave: "Why do you think you're here?"

Member: "Because we've been bad" (said sarcastically as laughter erupted from the group).

Dave (sensing some energy): "Do you agree, you've been bad?"

For the next ten minutes or so, I heard why the behavior of the team was not their fault. External circumstances just made it impossible to behave.

Dave: "So let me ask you this: If you all decide to keep 'being bad,' what do you think will happen?"

Member: "Some of us won't be here" (spoken with conviction and some frustration toward the group).

Dave: "Do you all want to be here?"

Members: "It's not about us."

Dave (interrupting now): "Actually, my question is about you. With everything you know about this place, do you want to be here?" (Silence)

Dave: "Do you want to be here?"

Members: "Ya, Dave, we do but . . ."

Dave: "No more buts."

Members: "Yes—we want to be here" (all but two of the group members shook their heads affirmatively).

Dave: "Okay, so my next question is this: Are you willing to make your team" (they were not yet a tribe) "and this place better? I understand you can't control everything, but are you willing to change what you can?"

Member: "Like what?"

For the next few minutes I shared my thoughts (based on their comments). We discussed what they could change—starting with a pretty foul attitude. They agreed with my assessment, though not always happy with me, and did admit there were ways to change.

Dave: "You have to want this. If you don't want it, this won't change. So, I want to ask all of you, are you willing to engage in a process that can lead you to change?" (I looked at the person just to my right.)

Person just to my right: "You mean you want me to tell you right now?"

Dave: "Yes. I want you to say 'I'm in' or 'I'm not.'"

Member: "Can we say, 'I don't know?'"

Dave: "Yes. But, within one week you have to change that answer to 'I'm in' or 'I'm not.'"

Member: "This is dumb."

Silence.

Silence.

Staring.

I've learned at these points not to talk but to let those types of statements sit for a moment. I didn't have to talk. Three of the members of the group asked the wavering member why he felt that way. They began to convince him to try to make it work. Then it happened. I love when it happens. It's one of my favorite things to watch. The members forgot I was there and began to engage each other in the conversation about possible solutions to their team dysfunctions.

I looked at the clock. "Fifty-five minutes in, not bad," I thought.

The third process step in Tribal Alchemy process is engagement. Alchemy happens, in part, because of emotional and strategic engagement in the challenge or opportunity. The quality of alchemy is linked to the quality of engagement. By engagement, I don't mean extraverted outbursts (although they are okay), I don't mean loud music that hypes the crowd (although there's a place for that), and I don't mean obsessive cheerleading that is as disingenuous as a fake potted plant. By engagement, I mean that a tribe is emotionally and strategically committed to the ingenious advancement of challenges and opportunities. Let's take a look.

We talk a lot about the power of emotion. We talk a lot about the power of strategy. Now we need to talk about how each one—emotion and strategy—affect the other.

The word *engage* has an interesting history and set of meanings. Think about it; you can engage someone to do something for you. This kind of engagement is a solicitation of sorts for the expertise of the other. The word can also connote your own participation in a project, event, or circumstance. *Engage* then is about inviting others or involving yourself. When I use the word here, I mean both. Engagement occurs when tribal members focus their actions, emotions, mind-sets, and strategies toward their challenges and opportunities. Each element (actions, emotions, mind-sets, and strategies) by itself is important but limited in its power. It is the combination of the elements that creates engagement. And tribal engagement increases the likelihood and quality of alchemy.

Before we look at each element in process step three, consider these two important ideas.

Important Idea Number One: Engagement Is Tribal, Not Just Individual

I don't want to play with semantics, but there is a difference between individual and tribal engagement. You could argue that for tribes to be engaged, individuals must also be engaged. And you would be right. However, individuals within a tribe can be engaged without that vibe transferring to the entire tribe. This causes frustration, sometimes both for the engaged and the disengaged. When only a small percentage of tribe members are engaged in alchemy, it can deflate those involved and irritate the disinterested. It's difficult for a few brave souls to shift the tribal culture. In some instances it can be done, but it takes patience and persistence.

A number of years ago, I spend quite a bit of time writing at a particular Starbucks in the city where I lived. The interesting thing about this Starbucks was that adjacent to the Starbucks was an Einstein Bros. Bagels. The two stores shared a common café space in the middle. It was perfect for me; I would grab my Starbucks and then a bagel and sit in the middle of the two stores where heaven and earth met. It only took a couple of months to notice the severe difference between the staff at the Starbucks and the staff at the Einstein Bagels. I could count on the staff of the Starbucks to be friendly, passionate about their work, and generally speaking, fun to be around. They seemed to like each other and enjoyed how they created alchemy with their customers. It was another story over at Einstein Bagels. It's not that the employees were angry or belligerent, but it was obvious they were not engaged in their work.

One of my favorite moments that demonstrated this lack of engagement occurred each time fresh bagels were taken out of the large ovens. Based on the ritual that would unfold, I surmised that a few Einstein Bagels executives must have attended a workshop at the famed Seattle Fish Market. In an attempt to build that Seattle Fish Market camaraderie among the Einstein Bagels employees, they adopted a mantra that would be initiated by the baker when he pulled bagels out of the oven and then repeated by the rest of the employees—a kind of call and response. If you've ever been to the Seattle Fish Market, you know that the employees sing a call and response at times as they work. The point of this call and response is just to encourage people to remain engaged and present to their work.

The mantra—chosen by the Einstein Bagel leaders—was "fresh hot bagels." Now, try to put yourself in the scene. You are sitting at a table in the common area with the Einstein Bagels behind you. You hear the oven doors open, and bagels come rolling out. At that point, the baker, with great enthusiasm, is to yell out, "Fresh hot bagels." Then, with the same level of passion, and in unison, the Einstein Bagels crew is to repeat,

"Fresh hot bagels." Again, the idea of this is to create an engagement and awareness in the employees and the general energetic environment that rubs off on the customers. Well, at the particular Einstein Bagels I frequented, the mantra "fresh hot bagels" should have been replaced with "crash and burn." The first problem originated with the baker. Instead of walking over to the door, pulling out the bagels, and yelling the mantra, he crawled over to the door in what seemed like a sleep-induced coma, opened the oven door, slowly rolled the bagels out of the oven in a zombie-like state, and in a monotone voice eked out the phrase "fresh hot bagels."

As you can imagine, this lack of passion signaled the crew to respond in kind. In fact, over time, I realized that only new employees, not yet savvy to the cultural norms, responded at all. After a few weeks, they too became chameleons and blended into the passionless vibe of the crew. Occasionally, a couple of workers would try to revive some energy, but it was very difficult due to the entropy of the entire tribe. One or two engaged individuals weren't enough to push the tribe into collective involvement. A tipping point was needed. That tipping point came when a new manager was hired to oversee the place and turn around the store. I watched her model engagement and require it of the tribe. Within a few months, one by one, tribe members said the mantra with greater passion until collective momentum was palpable.

What was also palpable was the newfound ability to alchemize that came as a result of the engagement. I noticed the Einstein Bagel employees acting more like the Starbucks employees. They not only seemed happier but more involved with their customers—looking for ways to enhance the experience of the patrons. I even noticed customers occasionally joining in with the crew when it was time to say the mantra. Engagement was no longer a gimmick but now an authentic expression of the tribe, and it leaked out and influenced the customers as well.

The idea of tribal engagement is tricky. For starters, size matters. It's easier to see the effects of engagement or disengagement when the tribe is smaller. Engagement is much harder to evaluate when the tribe is large.

It often takes a crisis or other type of dramatic intervention to shift the engagement level of large tribes, as in multinational corporations or nations, for instance. It also takes more time to reveal malaise and align around the work required to reverse disengagement. This is why global challenges are still best solved by local tribes (all over the globe) all working for the same change.

How many tribe members does it take to reach tribal engagement? Is there a critical mass, or does everyone have to be engaged? If one person isn't engaged, does that end tribal engagement? I recognize these are difficult and, maybe in some ways, impossible questions to answer. What we do know is that we, as human beings, affect each other in tangible ways. Moods, mind-sets, actions, and strategies are influential and shape tribal effectiveness. When we speak of engagement in the next pages, we are speaking of that qualitatively unique experience that occurs when people act, think, emote, and strategize together.

Important Idea Number Two: Engagement Is Not a Gimmick although Sometimes It Is Dressed Up Like One

There has been so much written about engagement and its importance in the pursuit of mission—some of it very good, some of it not. Because of the plethora of ideas on this subject, it's important first to define what I don't mean by *engagement*. Tribal engagement is not about hype. It is not about gimmicks to fire people up (although there are times and places to do such firing up). Tribal engagement is not about putting on that plastic smile when everything is terrible. Nor is it about saying things are "great" when they're falling apart. It's not about illusions of grandeur under very tight limitations, nor is it about simply being overly extroverted—through the waving of hands and boisterous tones—in a meeting or conversation. In other words, tribal engagement is not a disingenuous approach to tough times. Instead, tribal engagement combines authentic optimism with unapologetic realism. When action, emotion, mind-set, and strategy intersect with authentic optimism and unapologetic realism, engagement increases. Let's take a deeper look at what comes at the intersection of action, emotion, mind-set, and strategy.

. . .

The tribe had been meeting for three hours. In that time, it had overcome areas of disagreement and conflict, set a new course for its organization, and agreed upon initial strategies to set it all in motion. It was lunchtime. As the facilitator, I was proud of the tribe's effort and was energized by its cohesion and productivity. As we ate lunch, people talked to each other in collegial tones. There was laughter and a sense of camaraderie.

Just as lunch was wrapping up, I noticed a man walk into the room in a hurried manner. He loosened his tie and grabbed a sandwich. I glanced back at the group, most of whom had not seen the man arrive. The few tribe members that had seen him come in the room shot fast glances at each other—the kind of glance that suggests they were not happy with his entrance or his presence. Because everyone else was engaged in lunch, I went up to the man and introduced myself. "Hi, I'm Dave. I've been facilitating the retreat, and I just wanted to introduce myself to you."

"Oh, so you're Fleming, huh? Well I'll have you know that most of the people you've been working with this morning don't do strategic planning for a living. But I do. So this afternoon might be a bit more challenging for you, since I know what I'm doing."

I felt my gut tightening and my mind race with things I wanted to say but had the good fortune not to. Instead, I smiled and said, "Well, hopefully this afternoon will be as productive, and I look forward to learning with and from you."

A couple of the other tribe members overheard the exchange I had with the new arrival. One of them quietly came up to me. "Sorry about that Dave. Joe can get kind of full of himself. Just ignore him. We all do," she said with an uncomfortable laugh.

As lunch ended, we settled in for the afternoon. The energy was high, and anticipation was in the room. I spent a couple of minutes reviewing what had occurred in the morning. Heads were shaking with affirmation; that is, all but one. "You've got to be kidding. You actually think we can pull these things off?" You guessed it. The comment came from the late arrival. For the next 15 minutes, the tribe tried to bring him up to speed but to no avail. With each piece that they tried to help him understand, his objections became stronger and more emotionally volatile. "You know in my work I would've never done it like Fleming did it this morning." He explained to his colleagues how he would have used a much more effective method for the day. He was impressed, it seemed, with his ideas, though no one else appeared all that interested. I gently directed the conversation away from the new arriver and back onto the task at hand. He didn't seem pleased but was unable to sway the tribe in his direction. Though the tribe did regain focus, the energy in the room decreased each time the new arriver spoke. A mere 15 to 20 minutes into the afternoon, after a morning of hard and inspiring work, tribe members had lost their momentum and inspiration—something I spent the afternoon helping them regain.

What happened?

Mood Inductors

In her 2002 study "The Ripple Effect: Emotional Contagion and Its Influence on Group Behavior," Sigal G. Barsade called human beings "walking mood inductors." What a great description of human beings and the emotional influence we have on each other. We know that inductors are devices that temporarily store energy in the form of a magnetic field. I'll let you Google the word if you'd like to learn more, but it's a great metaphor to describe what human beings do with emotions. We are temporary storage units for emotions, not just our own, but the emotions conveyed by other tribe members. The tribe in the last example was affected by one man's emotional contagion. It changed the texture of the meeting and slowed progress. I knew that without an intentional intervention that was both realistic and positive, the afternoon would not look anything like the morning. Soon after the deflating comments, I decided the tribe and I needed a time out. We took a break. During the break, I assembled the leaders and the late arriver. We talked about our strategy for the afternoon. I included the late arriver in the conversation and implored him to work with us (and me) to make the afternoon as productive as the morning. He was willing to do this, though at times there were still bumps when he would speak. However, as he perceived he was valued, his loud and proud tone changed. He held onto less toxic emotional contagions and joined the tribe.

Barsade found that emotions are *contagions* and effect both collective performance and energy. When a tribe circles, it's easy to underestimate the power of tribal emotions both on the mood and strategic productivity. It only takes one powerful emotional contagion to shift an entire meeting, strategy, or initiative. Unnecessary and often unproductive swings in direction can be the result of the giving and receiving of emotions. That giving and receiving is happening whether we acknowledge it or not. Over three decades of working with tribes, I've noticed that effective tribes, and their leaders, are not afraid to recognize how emotions are influencing a moment or a process. They do this because they know that great possibilities can be undone when powerful emotions negatively consume the moment. What ingenious tribes also know is that emotions can increase engagement and effectiveness as much as they can derail them. The question is not should we allow emotion to influence engagement, but rather how can emotion influence engagement in both positive and realistic ways. Here are three ideas your tribe can use to leverage the power of emotional contagions often stored in the inductors of tribe members:

- Monitor emotional contagions as they occur
- Integrate emotional contagions into the conversation
- Find the good energy and layered strategy in the contagion

Monitor Emotional Contagions as They Occur

Too often, as strong emotional contagions occur, they are not well navigated by the tribe. A basic mindfulness about neurobiology comes in handy at this moment. When people display high levels of emotion, it can cause feelings of threat. We know, from biology, that when we feel threatened we respond in one of four ways. First, we may fight back in order to establish some control and security. Second, we may flee in order to regain security through isolation and protection. Third, we may freeze, unable to do or say anything. Or fourth, we may flock to safety in those who seem sympathetic to us, or just nearby.

These very basic primal drives that occur during threats also occur in the pursuit of alchemy. When we care deeply about mission, challenges, and opportunities, emotions can run high. When they do, it's very easy to display those emotions in strong and controlling ways. This display of emotion can throw other tribe members into their own place of threat. This moment of high threat is a very important moment in the life of a tribe. How the tribe handles the strong emotional contagion of one or more members is critical to its ability to remain engaged in alchemy. This moment, at the intersection of strong emotion and fear, is not necessarily a moment to avoid. In fact, it can be useful in shaping the tribe's actions.

If a tribe cannot work through strong emotion that elicits fear and threat, its alchemy will diminish, if not completely vanish. The reason this moment is so critical is that it is the moment when engagement either increases or is lost for good in the pursuit of alchemy. There is a great energy in this moment. Tribes that can appropriately navigate to the other side find an even greater amount of energy with which to move forward. Tribes that stall, shrink back, or run away from emotional activation will also find it hard to engage the messiness associated with challenges and opportunities.

This is why tribes must monitor contagions as they occur. Alchemy-producing tribes call these moments out and face them. The disagreements that lead to strong emotional contagions and the feeling of fear and threat must become part of the conversation of change, rather than that which ends it. As a facilitator, one of my most important roles with the tribe is to help them navigate these moments. I wish I could say I've always done a good job, but I haven't because I too have been drawn into the emotional contagions reaction and responded with my own version of fight, flight, flee, or flock. However, when I have been able to remain what psychologist call the non-anxious third party, I have seen tribes navigate strong emotion and fear in very powerful ways. This leads to greater engagement and greater alchemy. A note of caution is important here. These are tricky waters. The ability to monitor strong emotion requires tribal trust. Your tribe may not be ready to engage at this level. More basic trust building may be necessary before venturing out into these types of conversations. But effective tribes learn to monitor and speak about emotional contagions and the strong reactions they produce as they happen, not later in the parking lot when the meeting is over. Monitor well.

Integrate Emotional Contagion into the Conversation

Once your tribe has identified a strong emotional contagion linked to threat or fear, it's then important to integrate these contagions into the conversation. This is where the beauty of a tribe can really shine. It's rare for every person in a tribe to simultaneously feel the same level of emotional contagion and/or reaction to that contagion. Some members are normally not as activated as others. At this time, a kind of mutual regulation of the moment is needed. Psychologists and psychiatrists have helped us to understand the power of emotional regulation and what they call coregulation. Coregulation is the ability we have to help each other find calm and mindfulness in the midst of stress and angst. Once contagions have been identified, less activated members can support healthy equilibrium in a positive and affirming way. Not only that, but the conversation around the challenge or the opportunity can then include an evaluation of the strong emotional reactions. Questions like "Why are we activated right now?" "What is it about this part of the conversation that has caused these kinds of reactions?" and others can enable a tribe to learn from, rather than run from, their contagions.

There are times that emotional reactions are simply the result of selfish agendas or petty disagreements. However, much of the time emotional contagions are likely the result of passionate people sharing ideas they believe in. This is a good thing, even when it's wrapped in strong emotion. Strong emotion in a tribe should signal to the tribe members that they are near important content. That content—and those tribe members—should be handled with respect. Less activated members of the tribe should coregulate and help the tribe restore calm while simultaneously encouraging the tribe to look at the content motivating their reactions.

I was recently with a tribe that was discussing an important part of its mission. As they were discussing, the conversation turned toward one particular and important initiative. This initiative was critical to the success of the organization and its ability to sustain itself financially. At one point, the leader said with strong emotional force, "If we don't get this right we won't have to worry about anything, because we won't be here." A couple of people in the tribe shook their heads in agreement while others seem to disengage in that moment.

I stopped the leader and asked if that was indeed true. Was it true that failure around this particular initiative would lead to everyone losing their jobs? I looked at the leader and said, "I'm not sure I think that's really true, and if it's not, it's not fair to say. So can you share if indeed it is?"

I saw the leader swallow hard and become more vulnerable. At that point she masterfully explained how her emotion had mixed with fear and, to some degree, with reality. This mixture had crated an unfair statement. She reflected, "I have to admit my statement was driven somewhat by fear, and I need to reframe it. Let me say it this way: the success of this initiative will enable us to continue our work and prove to those around us that we are legitimate. I do think failure would hurt our ability to continue our mission, but it's not right to say that everyone would lose their job. I said that out of fear, but I don't want to discount the importance of this moment and this particular initiative."

At the end of her comments, the tribe was energized and understood the mandate she had given and was more fully engaged in meeting it. I witnessed this leader do a brilliant job of integrating the emotional contagion into the moment in a way that made the heightened emotions a positive part of the conversation rather then the element that would shut it down. This particular leader is one of the best leaders I know. Her willingness to be vulnerable in appropriate ways, and yet still remain confident in her leadership, was in part why this moment increased engagement. A lesser leader could have easily shut down my comment and reinforced his or her own viewpoint with an even stronger emotional reaction. I've seen it done many times. I've done it myself many times. Because the leader was willing to be vulnerable in the moment of the reaction, the emotional contagion became part of engaging the tribe more deeply into its work. Sometimes it's important to explain the emotion orbiting the content because it sheds light on the content and the content giver.

Find the Strategy in the Contagions and Layer Them Together

Once you have monitored a contagion and a reaction to it, and integrated it into the conversation, you can then find the strategies attached to it that can both engage the tribe and further your alchemy. A number of years ago I was working with the board from a nonprofit organization. They asked me to come spend the day with them as they thought about the next two years of their organization. During the meeting, one gentleman took on the role of naysayer. In a respectful manner, he contradicted many of the ideas put forth by the board as we moved through the strategic agenda. I could almost predict at what times, during the day, he was going to speak. Beyond that, after a few comments, when he spoke, it was a foregone conclusion his comments would contradict whatever was the predominant or prevailing view. This type of tribe member can cause enormous frustration for a tribe. However, I've learned over the years to value these voices because they often contain important ideas missing from the predominant view. The problem is that these members often deliver their thoughts in frustrating or irritating ways, which causes others to dismiss both the person and the attached ideas. I saw this happening to the board member at the retreat.

As the day progressed, when he would speak, eyes would roll and audible sighs could be heard in the room. At a critical moment of decision, he stopped the conversation and expressed his dismay over a choice the board was about to make. The rest of the tribe felt energized and ready to make the decision and move forward. He, on the other hand, reacted more strongly to this moment than any other during the day. I stopped the flow of conversation and addressed the contrarian. "I want you to know I appreciate your voice," I said to him. "I know you have some concerns about the financial stability of the organization, and I'm not sure you feel heard about that." As I spoke, he sat up and looked at me as if to say, "Finally, someone is hearing me." "I also know," I said, "that the majority of the board feels it's time to make this decision about the financial direction of the organization. I want your voice to be a part of this conversation, but I don't want your voice to hijack this conversation. Do you agree?" He shook his head in the affirmative. "Can you share in just a couple of sentences with your colleagues your major concerns?"

He looked down for a moment and then back up. In two sentences he articulated his concern and even his solution to his concern. No one had thought of his solution, and it absolutely made the larger decision a better one. One by one, the rest of the board members affirmed this gentleman's idea and even thanked him for his willingness to object with respect. Not only did the tribe experience more engagement as a result of this moment, but the actual strategy was more robust because it added a perspective that was needed.

Often when emotional contagions are strong, there is also an important piece of strategy lurking nearby. Just because someone has a strong emotional reaction and is irritating in the delivery doesn't mean they don't have a good idea. It also doesn't automatically mean that they have a great idea. Smart tribes are able to "nuance out" the idea and separate it from the emotion. However, it's the emotion that often signals that the tribes should stop and pay attention to the idea wrapped in the strong reaction.

I want to state clearly that strong reactions don't always contain brilliant strategies. Sometimes we just overreact and need to be co-regulated back to a place of calm. We don't need to be coddled if the moment doesn't happen to go our way. However, I firmly believe that more times than not, strong emotional contagion, and the reactions that come as a result, signal to the tribe that it's time to slow down, pay attention, go deeper into the moment, and search for "the better" hidden in "the difficult." By monitoring and integrating emotions into these moments, the tribe can become more engaged in the process of alchemy and in the process of developing strong and effective tribal bonds.

Remember the professionals and door number one, two, and three? Part of the reason I asked them to choose a door was to help them take individual responsibility for their actions. However, there was another reason equally as important. Their chosen door would also shape their mind-set. If you remember, door number two was about authentic optimism and unapologetic realism. Door number two, like the other doors, was also a *mind-set*. I asked them to *choose* their mind-set because that mind-set would influence both the type and degree of their engagement. Think about it: door number one (which was to stay and complain) would only increase a dysfunctional mind-set and lead to apathy and lethargy. Door number two, however, would *shift mind-set*. Of course, not every problem would go away just because people chose door number two. On the contrary, some problems could grow worse because denial and perpetual complaining would no longer be an option. I knew any increase in alchemy was related to an increase in an optimistic and realistic mind-set.

The same is true for every tribe. Much research has been done on mind-set. The way in which we see situations affects, to some degree, how they will turn out. That's not an absolute statement. Sometimes mind-set doesn't change the outcome, but it often does significantly influence it. We cannot ignore its importance. This section is not a deep exploration of mind-set. For a powerful exploration of mind-set, I would direct you to the work of Harvard psychologist Ellen Langer. Langer's work is at times counterintuitive, but it is well grounded in substantive research and sound thought. Her experiments reveal why perspective matters greatly with regard to any type of performance. However, there are those who caution against a misuse or overemphasis on the role of a growth-oriented mind-set.

In an August 2015 *Salon* article, "The Perils of 'Growth Mind-set' education: Why We're Trying to Fix Our Kids When We Should Be Fixing the System," Alfie Kohn, education reformer, warned against a view of mind-set that overemphasizes one element of effectiveness to the exclusion of others. For instance, he pointed out that simply telling kids they are "smart" in hopes that such a mind-set will influence their performance, is short sighted and even dangerous. A child's mind-set about her intelligence level isn't the only issue that contributes to excellence in education. To suggest to kids that all barriers are overcome through a personal growth mind-set is a mischaracterization of the complexity of learning and education. The same is true of any alchemy. Simply believing that your tribe will achieve great alchemy doesn't make it so. However, the way you think does affect the quality of alchemy. So, mind-set isn't just about *what we already are,* but it's also about *what we desire to be, do, and make with our raw materials.* Mind-set is aspirational in that it *positions us to behave in certain ways* as we arrive at the magic-making moment (as well as during it).

For our purposes let's consider two important tribal dynamics that influence mind-set. First, craft noble tribal mind-sets. And second, return to the noble mind-sets as soon as you recognize you've left them.

Craft Noble Mind-Sets

As we've seen, the prevailing mind-set of your tribe matters. Of course, mind-sets fluctuate with the moods and situations. It's important to recalibrate mind-sets in real time. However, it's equally important, if not more important, to establish noble mind-sets that shape your tribal culture. We've been talking about this idea for decades now. In the 1980s and early 1990s we spoke of vision and the importance of having one that compelled a tribe forward. We added to that the importance of values—a set of agreed-upon ways we will think, act, and feel together. Vision and values are still important, although we've overused both words and, in doing so, diminished the meaning of both. When I speak of crafting noble mind-sets, I'm speaking of something a bit different than vision and values, although it's related.

Noble mind-sets describe how tribes will both view and engage challenges and opportunities. My work and in-the-field-research with tribes has revealed that a significant difference between a magic-making and a magic-breaking tribe is the *mind-set they bring to the moment of challenge or opportunity*. The ingenious tribes have noble mind-sets already in place as the challenge or opportunity emerges. Why? Because these tribes know that once a challenge or opportunity emerges, it's much harder to shift to noble mind-sets if you have not already established them. Challenges and opportunities reveal mind-sets that are already established. This is why crafting them before is essential to success and enhances engagement.

Tribes need to create *mind-set mantras* that reflect how they want to behave when challenges and opportunities surface. These statements need to reflect the noblest part of collective humanity. They also need to be authentic in that the tribe regularly practices and talks about them. They are a part of the tribe's way of being. Here are some examples of noble mind-set mantras:

- We believe in the collective genius of our tribe.
- We believe that our collective genius will help us overcome challenge and maximize opportunity.
- We value each other.
- We believe in each other and know that when we combine our skills and insights, our engagement and alchemy increases.
- During times of challenge and difficulty, we will integrate emotion without being hijacked by it.
- During times of opportunity we will make wise choices and align around core and needed efforts.

The mantras above are likely too long. Your tribe would have to agree to the concept and then cut the words down to something even shorter than the phrases above. For example, number two could be trimmed down to "collective genius in the challenge." This is easier to remember and is more usable in moments when brevity matters. The fifth sentence could be trimmed down to "don't hijack, integrate."

. . .

As you can see, the statements above are aspirational—an important quality in noble mind-sets. During challenges and opportunities, we would never aspire to implode or fail as a tribe. However, failure and implosion happens all too often, partly because no noble mind-set mantras are used to elevate the tribe during challenging times.. In fact, many tribes have a plethora of ignoble mantras they use during challenges and opportunities, not realizing they assist in the demise of their alchemy. Still, at this point, you might be thinking, "Really? You want us to create and say mantras? Should we sit in a circle and hold hands as well?" The notion of creating and using mantras during times of challenges and opportunity or, for that matter, during any kind of moment, may seem unnecessary and even ridiculous. It might feel like something you could have seen on an episode of *The Office*. But before you dismiss this idea, consider this. What appeals to us about an inspirational speech given by a coach during a difficult moment in a game? Why, when we experience this moment, do we feel something surge inside us? Why do companies spend millions, if not billions, of dollars, on their brands, specifically on the small descriptive phrases they want you to remember? Why do teams huddle before, during, and after games? Why do they often finish a huddle with a small mantra spoken by all of them?

It's undeniable that words create meaning and meaning shapes action. The same is true for your tribe during times of challenge and opportunity. Mind-set mantras rally the tribe around noble ideas and behaviors that are important to alchemy. Though you may have to overcome some internal and emotional resistance, once you do, you will find your tribe more energized because its members are more in line with both how they want to behave and what they want to create.

Align Action Again and Again

You know those moments in life when you just don't care? You know, right? Your mind-set goes south, and pretty soon so does your action. For example, I can think of many days when I have awakened with a plan to exercise after my workday. But the trials of the day, and the resulting psychological and emotional funk I create, affect my after-work actions. Instead of exercising, I chose something easier, like eating ice cream or just staring at a screen. Mind-set affects behavior. The good news is that the opposite is also possible. There are many days when we choose noble mind-sets that lead to more effective action. Sometimes this is a hard choice to make. And, for a bit of time, we're not sure it's worth it. The "Oh, why in the world should I care?" syndrome can pull like a riptide. But if we prevail toward more noble mind-sets, we often pick up momentum. It becomes easier to act out those better desires. This idea is also important for tribes.

When a tribe's mind-sets elevate toward noble aspirations, its action is affected. A tribe's decision to embrace noble mind-sets influences the quality of collective behavior. I don't know what specific actions and behaviors are important to your tribe's mission and alchemy. The actions of a tribe, in some ways, point to the unique mission it expresses in the world. What is consistent, though, from tribe to tribe is the interplay between mind-set and action.

Consider basketball as an example. During the course of a game, the energy and effective action of a team ebbs and flows. When the energy ebbs, it's not unlikely for the opposing team to score several baskets in short order. The momentum shifts and the lethargic team finds itself in trouble—sometimes in big trouble, with thousands of opposing fans celebrating their trouble. A downward mind-set can take over. Sometimes you can even see this mind-set through the posture and actions of the deflated team. This is a critical moment in the game. It's a moment where coaches often must intervene to stop the slide. What does the coach do at a time like this? I've watched basketball for a good portion of my life, and I've noticed a predictable strategy employed by coaches. When a team's mind-set and actions slide for more than a couple of minutes, the coach calls a timeout.

Timeouts due to ineffectiveness, allow the coach to take a couple of important actions. First, he or she reconnects the team to their more noble mind-sets. The coach may give a pep talk that links mind-set to action. The content of the pep talk varies depending on how the team is underperforming. Some coaches may need to increase the level of energy, while at other times, the coach may need to slow his team down. When a coach intervenes, he or she reminds the team about nobler mind-sets and how to reconnect their action to them. The coach looks for a way to get the team to care again, because more noble mind-sets have the potential to transform less effective action. If your tribe wants to engage in alchemy, it needs to connect its behavior with its most noble mind-sets, not once, but again and again. When you lose that connection, a timeout is in order. When the connection is reestablished, and engagement increases, alchemy is more likely.

Connect Your Actions to Your Noble Mind-Sets, Again and Again

In the world of meditation, seasoned practitioners and teachers all talk about distraction, which we could define as a loss of connection to more noble mind-sets. It seems that, if you're going to meditate, you're going to face distractions. In my own meditation and teaching of meditation, I believe the distractions should not be viewed as a negative but rather as an early warning signal that you've lost your center and that it's time to return. Meditation teachers of all stripes advise that when you recognize distraction in the midst of your meditation, you should simply return to the word, phrase, or object of your meditation. Instead of being frustrated by the distraction, you should see it as a signal to return to that nobler place. This is a great example of how tribes can utilize lesser mind-sets to move them back to better actions.

When a tribe is in the middle of a challenge/opportunity, they can lose touch with their more noble mind-sets. The normal course of challenges and opportunities pulls tribe members away from their better selves just like my situations pulled me from my intention to exercise. This is to be expected. During these less-than moments, tribes, just like meditators, should return to their more noble mind-sets crafted before the challenge/opportunity emerged. If your tribe notices its mind-set sliding south, simply return to the more noble statements and reconnect your collective behavior to them. This idea takes us back to an earlier insight about attention. When we pay attention to our actions *while we act*, the quality of those actions increases. Mindfulness about action makes that action better. For a tribe, then, it must rally its attention back around its noble mind-sets of engagement. This reminder ignites better action, which leads to more engagement. The quality of action increases the quality of engagement, and the quality of engagement increases the quality of action.

I suggest the more noble aspirations should be written down. This makes it easier to return to them when distractions overtake the circle. Coming back (returning) to the more noble aspirations engages the tribe to behave in ways that reflect their deeper desires. That engagement is critical to alchemy.

Strategy Matters

In a sense, I suppose you could say that Tribal Alchemy is a strategic design framework. However, there are other models more specifically focused on crafting strategies and/or designing projects and initiatives in a collaborative fashion. Harvard Business School and the Institute of Design at Stanford are two good places to start your exploration if you're looking for more information about either strategy or design. The big idea I want to convey here is that strategy and design are forms of tribal engagement. We tend to see both as ways to enhance the quality of an object or subject in the world. And that is certainly true. Strategies and design techniques do enable alchemy in powerful ways. However, they also enable engagement, which is often overlooked by tribes when performing either function.

I've spent years working with networks of tribes who are together trying to make a difference in their world. When tribes join forces they can increase and maximize energy and output. However, what I've noticed over the years of working with tribes around collective action is this:

When tribes are left out of the strategy or design elements of the work,
they are less engaged in the downstream action.

When a tribe enters an initiative late in the game or is for some reason left out of the circle of strategic planning and design, it is less engaged in the execution of the work. If you want to increase your tribe's engagement around any challenge or opportunity, ensure the members are part of both the strategic thinking and the ongoing design and redesign as the work unfolds. When you're expected to perform but are left out of these key elements, engagement rapidly degenerates into compliance or worse.

We tend to think of strategy and design as elements that occur early in the work of challenge or opportunity. However, we all know that adaptation is critical to ongoing success. Therefore, if a tribe, or some of its members, is disengaged in the midst of a challenge and/or opportunity, it's important to bring them into the redesign process in order to engage them in the work. It is in the *doing of strategy and design* that tribal members increase emotional investment and engagement. To overlook this important dynamic is to miss out on the possibility of greater iterations of alchemy. When engagement is low or waning, do the following:

- Invite the disengaged to a conversation around strategy.
- Invite the disengaged to rethink certain design elements of the challenger and/or opportunity.
- Invite the disengaged to work on a specific area of the challenge or opportunity that needs better strategy or design.
- Listen and incorporate the ideas of the disengaged as possible.
- Be honest with the disengaged when you cannot use their ideas and keep them in the circle as the work continues.

It does not escape me that some disengaged tribe members have bad attitudes. As you work to engage them by including them in strategy and design, you may also have to challenge them to reconnect to more noble mind-sets. Tribal members are often more likely to aspire to noble mind-sets when they have a reason to do so. Inviting the disengaged to the circle of strategy and design gives them a reason to do so. We all desire to feel needed and valued. Often, because of bad attitudes, the disengaged are devalued and disenfranchised. Tribal leaders often want the disengaged to change their attitude *before* they will give them any responsibility. There are times that this is a wise strategy. However, there are other times when attitudes shift once the invitation to join has been given. Not all disengaged tribe members are cranky for no good reason. Sometimes disengaged tribe members feel disenfranchised because they've not been invited to make a difference. The best tribes, and the best tribal leaders, look to activate energy by giving the disengaged a reason to care and bring their better selves forward. However, this invitation to the table of strategy and design is not without responsibility. Bad attitudes around the table can demolish engagement and end alchemy. This is why the disengaged must be invited with a challenge to engage in positive and realistic ways. Give the disengaged a reason to do so, challenge them to rise above petty attitudes, and they just might surprise you.

Watch for the POP

Remember autostereograms? They come back into play during engagement. When a tribe is in the midst of challenge or opportunity and they bring their best thinking and feeling to the process, they must then look for and expect the POP. The POP is the moment when the raw materials are organized in such a manner that the "better" reveals itself. BOOM. The collective *aha* is an extremely powerful moment. Use it. Seize it. Let the energy of it move you to the next actions of alchemy. It takes engagement to see the pop, and it creates engagement once the pop occurs. Watch for it. Don't let the energy it creates dissipate too quickly. Use it to sustain the process toward the transformation you desire.

TRANSFORM

A Singing Tribe

Eric Whitacre, known for his beautiful choral compositions and innovative video choirs, began a TED talk by declaring, "I always wanted to be a rock star." In his talk, he recounted the hours he spent playing and programming synthesizers. He also recalled the day he joined a choir—a choice that forever altered him. Whitacre discovered he had a gift for choral composition. He honed his craft over many years and has become a prominent composer. He is now known around the world for his work. Whitacre's "virtual choirs" are some of his more innovative ideas. In an interview about the virtual choir, Whitacre shared its beginnings:

> It all started with this one young girl who sent me this video of herself singing one of my coral pieces. And I was struck so hard by the beauty, the intimacy of it, the sweetness of it . . . and I thought wouldn't it be amazing if we could get 100 people to do this and cut it altogether—a virtual choir. So I then went into a studio and I conducted in total silence. I

could only hear it in my head and I loaded all of that up to YouTube . . . and I sent out a call to singers across the world. . . and the response was totally overwhelming. We had a 185 singers from 12 different countries. It was all about connecting and about somehow connecting with these people all over the world. These individuals alone, together.

If you're unfamiliar with Whitacre's virtual choirs, members sing their vocal part of a choral piece into a camera and send it to Whitacre. He and a group of technicians then compile all of the videos into an amazing virtual choral experience. It is alchemy, indeed.

You can see some of Whitacre's virtual choirs on YouTube. I would suggest you begin with the first choir that sang his composition entitled *Lux*. After you watch the original virtual choir singing *Lux*, hold off before watching any other videos until you've read further into this chapter. I'll reference virtual choirs again and some of the other videos to watch.

Whitacre had a serendipitous revelation about the virtual choir that led to this singing tribe of unbelievable musical and virtual alchemy. At some point, the ingenious idea for the virtual choir had to move beyond a great idea and become a great manifestation. This move from the moment of insight to the moment of manifestation is what occurs in the fourth process step of alchemy. The raw materials are transformed by the action of the tribe. Until your tribe *actualizes ideas*, you don't have alchemy. Whether it's a choir, product, or service, alchemy requires the move from the unseen to the concrete world (even if that concrete world is virtual).

Actions That Enable Transformation

Every tribe has unique raw materials that must be transformed through the skills of the tribe. Because I likely don't possess the skills of your tribe, I cannot speak to the specific way in which your raw materials are transformed. You and your tribe members have spent years learning how to create alchemy with and through your raw materials. For example, if a surgeon and her tribe (in the surgical suite) encountered a challenge that required alchemy, I would not be able to coach them on the clinical aspects needed to overcome the challenge. I don't have the skills. If a group of sound technicians encountered a challenge during a show and had to transform the gear they had to solve the problem they encountered, I would likely not understand how they did it. Some knowledge required for the transformation is unique because it is embedded in know-how, skill, and experience.

Regardless of the technical skills needed for your tribe to transform, there are common dynamics that all effective tribes utilize during transformative action. These actions enable the tribe to use its unique skills and raw materials in ingenious ways. No matter what your tribe does, these are behaviors that support the collective action of transformation. When tribes practice these common behaviors, even the quality and effectiveness of their unique skills can increase.

- Risk into creative action by opening up space for it.
- Stay through the inevitable tensions because that's where the alchemy is often hiding.
- Learn in order to create better and better alchemy and celebrate to create camaraderie and energy for more alchemy.

1. Risk Into Creative Action By Opening Up A Space For It: The Trapeze Artist

As a kid, my favorite part of the circus was the trapeze act. I would sit in anticipation and stare at the motionless swings. How would the flyer bring the trapeze to life? What tricks would she do? What dangers would he overcome? To this day, a trapeze act takes my breath away. I don't think I'm alone. The trapeze act is an amazing feat to watch. Beyond watching the trapeze artist, many individuals spend time and money learning the trapeze for themselves.

Why does the trapeze act so intrigue us? Is it because the artist can swing on a trapeze high above a crowd? Perhaps to some degree. But if that's all she did, we would quickly lose interest. Is it the "catch" that's made at the end of the acrobatic act? Again, the catch is amazing because of timing and trust. But the catch alone is not enough to sustain the attention of the crowd. When we watch the trapeze artist, we are mesmerized by the movements *in between* the swings. The most amazing movement of the trapeze comes as the artist risks letting go of *what is safe* so that she can perform her most creative act before landing in the arms of the catcher. Without that risk, all we would see is a person on a swing.

In the show *Ovo*, Cirque du Soleil artists took the trapeze to a new direction. They combined the trapeze act with stationary throws from a suspended platform. This fresh approach increased both the difficulty and the sensation of the act. You can watch the *Ovo* flying act on YouTube. It gives a great visual example of how flyers risk their way to creativity. Take a look at the video and as you watch it, and think of your tribe. In your own way, you too must risk out into *creative space* if you are to transform what you have into what you need. Though it can be unnerving, moments of risk activate possibility, which enables transformation.

Alchemy requires risk because transformation comes when we move beyond the familiar and act in different ways. Just as the trapeze artist must let go into empty space in order to create, so tribes must risk into the empty space of *ambiguity and uncertainty*. Without this risk, alchemy cannot occur. Virtual choir creator Eric Whitacre had no idea what he would receive when he sent his initial call out to the world. Nor could he predict how his new virtual tribe would sound together. There was no way to know how the technology would support his vision. The innovative idea was just an idea until Whitacre and others risked without knowing if and how the vision would manifest. This is true of all alchemy.

Once an alchemic idea reveals itself to a tribe, there is still no guarantee that it will lead to transformation. The transformational work of alchemy is still ahead. This is why ambiguity is part of the alchemy process. Your tribe *can't know before the work begins* if and how the transformation will occur. Sometimes you don't know until you are nearing the end of the creative action. This is why risk is an essential element of tribal transformations. Your tribe has to begin enacting ideas without guarantees.

Ingenious tribes let go of the first trapeze—the familiar—in order to venture out into the unknown where creativity is possible. The most creative time for a trapeze artist occurs when he has nothing to hold on to.

I call this the "midair moment."

The Midair Moment: The Space for Creative Action in the Midst of Uncertainty

I recently sat with the CEO of a company in transition. A series of significant decisions initiated a change in the organization that would require everyone involved to approach their work and their role in new ways. As we outlined some of these changes, it became evident that this tribe had entered a midair moment. With great passion, the CEO relayed his excitement about the future as he simultaneously shared his uncertainty about how to get there. "I really don't know today all of what this means, and I really don't know how I'm going to have to change so that this transition can occur. But what I do know is that I'm ready to make this journey because I believe in where we're headed and I know together we can get there."

For the next 30 minutes or so, the gathered tribe discussed the risk needed to create its future. As they talked, a sense of excitement and apprehension filled the room.

"Here we are," I thought to myself, "right at the *choice point* where a tribe must decide to risk into the creative space where they can create the change they desire."

I've seen many tribes reach the midair moment and shrink back in fear. I've seen others deliberate the wisdom of the risk and determine it wasn't time to risk. I've seen others risk, but with a lack of commitment that weakened their alchemic power. And I've seen other tribes risk with confidence (and humility) toward the transformation they believe in. Without this risk, the tribe will not be positioned correctly to rearrange what they have into what they need. Why? Because *without the risk, there is no need to transform much of anything.*

More on the Midair Moment and the Space for Alchemy

Alchemy requires space.

Tribes have to get their raw materials (and themselves) into a space where they can transform them. This space differs for tribes depending on what they do—what kind of mission they pursue. This space could be a literal space for creative action. Manoj Bhargava, founder of 5-Hour Energy Drink, uses his wealth to solve global issues. At his headquarters in Michigan, Manoj and his tribe built a building they named Stage 2 Innovations. Stage 2 Innovations is a literal space for alchemy where a tribe of engineers and tinkerers have the necessary margin to explore and experiment with raw materials. The results are impressive. They include a bicycle you ride for an hour, and it then generates electricity for 24 hours. What does it take to accomplish such innovation? Space to risk, fail, learn, and adapt.

Other tribes may not meet in a laboratory or an innovation building but may use a series of meetings or a retreat or even just a five-minute hallway conversation to create the space. Meetings have long been underutilized and are often dreaded spaces where tribes drone on about meaningless updates or launch into perpetual complaining. Smart tribes view meetings as innovation spaces where they meet to risk, design, deliberate, and transform.

The space created to risk differs from tribe to tribe. What is common, however, is the need for that *creative space that opens through risk*. When a trapeze artist lets go of the first swing, the space for creativity opens up. The "letting go" that enables space is a bold move whether you're on a trapeze or in the middle of creating alchemy with your tribe. When your tribe makes this move, it is energizing and often simultaneously unsettling. If you feel a little sick to your stomach or energized by the prospect, you've probably got yourself in a space where transformation can occur.

Think about it this way. As members of tribes, when we tell stories about transformation, *after the fact*, we often tell of midair moments as if they were the best parts of the work. Yet when we are in the midst of the midair moment, it's easy to disparage or rush through it because it is often a difficult and uncomfortable moment. We know in retrospect that the transformation would not have occurred without the risk into creative space. The hard and ingenious work that accompanies the risk is part of the necessary raw materials your tribe needs in order to transform the present into the future.

Recognize You're in a Midair Moment and Give It Its Due

Once tribes get to the process step of transformation, much work has already been done. They've seen a challenge or opportunity. They've named and engaged that challenge or opportunity. Now comes the transformation. By the time you arrive at the transformative action, it's easy to hurry the process to the end. Once we get an idea, we too often rush because it feels like we've already been at it for a long time. We want the end outcome. The trouble is that if we rush the transformative actions that lead to alchemy, we end up creating something lesser rather than better. It's in the *creative space* where the alchemy, and the other three process steps, must continue to work together in order to bring about the change we desire. Because of this, tribe members would do well to identify midair moments in order to embrace them more fully and mine them more deeply.

Once an idea moves to the creative action stage, the space needed for that work must take priority. Just as tribes must aspire to higher and more noble mind-sets, they must also aspire to and make room for the space of creative action. Eric Whitacre's dream of a virtual choir was only an idea until the creative space was made for the alchemic process to occur. Some tribes talk about alchemy but never get around to combining the raw materials in an ingenious way. As human beings we have an amazing ability to equate talking about something with doing it. Talking is critical. Dialogue is essential. But it is not enough. In order to transform raw materials we must make the space to work with them in different and novel ways. Of course we know this, but *the seeming urgencies of the day often divert the attention of the tribe away from the space required.* If your tribe wants to alchemize, you have to first recognize the midair moment has emerged and then *give it its due*. One way to spot if your tribe is serious about alchemy is to watch whether it gives space for the creative actions required. If tribe members say they want change but never make room for it, then what they've got is mostly hot air.

Learning to Recognize a Midair Moment: Questions to Ask as a Tribe

- Do you notice the clues and cues when you are approaching a midair moment? What might those be?
- During past midair moments, what dynamics preceded the midair moment? Lethargy? Apathy? Excitement? Lack of clarity? All these dynamics, plus many others, can be clues you're heading into a midair moment.
- Do you have regular time to discuss what you are noticing about current situational dynamics and the insights of tribe members?
- Do you honor the resistance that often comes during midair moments, or does your tribe back away from resistance in order to keep a pseudopeace?
- When you are in a midair moment—one that deserves time and space—does your tribe add it on to an already overloaded schedule, or do you make time for it by eliminating lesser priorities?
- Do you capture your tribal insights before, during, and after midair moments so they are accessible in and beyond the midair moment?
- What lessons from past midair moments can help you navigate the next ones with greater effectiveness?

2. Stay through The Inevitable Tensions Because That's Where The Alchemy Is Often Hiding.

Tension Is *Not* a Bad Word

In order for tribes to alchemize, they must reframe negative views about tension. We've already explored the importance of healthy tension, but we need to explore it a bit more because the midair moment is inherently a time of tension. Peter Senge, senior lecturer at MIT and author of the definitive work *The Fifth Discipline*, wrote, "The gap between vision and current reality is also a source of energy. If there were no gap, there would be no need for any action to move towards the vision. We call this gap creative tension" (p. 159).

Senge's description of the gap as creative tension is a positive frame indeed. However, it doesn't always feel positive when we hit the gap, the midair moment, because it's not always evident that the tension is leading the tribe to something transformative. And even if it is evident, it's still difficult to embrace tension because it requires that we navigate collective fears, anxieties, and situational uncertainties.

There's an instructive scene for us here at the end of the movie *The Lord of The Rings: The Fellowship of the Ring*. Leaders from the free peoples, not under the rule of the dark leader Sauron, assembled to discuss how to destroy Sauron's ring. If the ring falls back into his hands, he will achieve world domination. The group assembled is not yet a tribe (by my definition), but this scene is what moves them toward tribal action. As they try to decide what to do with the ring, tensions flair, prejudices arise, and accusations fly. Thoroughly negative frames dominate the conversation as the leaders consider options. As the tension heightens, Frodo, the hobbit who inherited the ring from Bilbo Baggins, stands up and quietly declares, "I will take the ring." Barely discernible over the yelling, he says it again until everyone is silently looking at him. "I will take the ring" he says, "though I do not know the way."

A midair moment inevitably brings tension. The stakes are high, the fears are real, and the future is uncertain. Because of this, we can quickly seek equilibrium—that is, to feel in control again. We get frustrated when things don't go our way or difficulties increase as we try to do good work. Yet the alchemy we seek comes from a disequilibrium we dislike—and often avoid through cleverly constructed strategies like yelling or name calling or silence or a hundred other possible actions. Ironically, as we try to reestablish control, we are losing what we want: a chance to create something better. Frodo could have walked away, remained silent, or joined the dysfunction around him. Instead, he moved deeper into the tension, stayed through it, and looked to find a way to provide a different way forward.

The Myth of Having Everything "Just So"

I've never been a big fan of the concept of life or work balance, for individuals or tribes. I should clarify that it's not the idea of balance as much as the way the concepts are shared that bugs me. The idea that an individual or tribe can distribute and sustain an equal amount of energy in all areas just doesn't make sense to me. For instance, over the last two days, other than the activities required for my survival, I've pretty much been focused on writing. I'm way out of balance. Or am I creating balance? Sometimes to seize an opportunity, tribes have to focus all their energy on one possibility, one set of actions.

What if, instead of viewing balance as a state of equal energy distribution across many domains, we saw balance as the skill of embracing and correcting necessary imbalances (or tensions)—kind of like riding a bike.

The Imbalance Intention of Bike Riding

About a year ago, my wife and I were riding our beach cruisers when I happened to notice a white line on the road. I decided to try to keep my bike perfectly centered on that white line. The line was no more than three or four inches wide and laid out in front of me for a few miles. As I rode that line, I noticed how difficult, actually impossible, it was for me to keep my bike perfectly centered and in balance with the white line. My inability to remain centered and balanced led me to an important insight. *Balance is not the elimination of imbalances but rather the correction of them.* In order to ride a bike (which is not easy to describe) you must continually correct small imbalances, small tensions that could derail you from your goal of staying on the bike. Therefore, balance requires imbalance. If you want the one (balance), you must navigate the other (imbalance). The two dynamics interrelate.

If you try to eliminate imbalance, or creative tension, from your tribe you also eliminate the possibility of transformation. The tension and the transformation work together to move a tribe along. Tribes that alchemize understand that tension and imbalance are important elements in the alchemic process. They embrace those elements as part of the way forward. Leaders and tribe members alike must remind each other that tension and imbalance are necessary dynamics and the pursuit of change. They must emulate Frodo by staying with the tension and providing a safe place to consider the value of the tension and how it could lead to transformation.

. . .

Here's a simple way to help your tribe value imbalance and tension. Spend some time discussing the following questions. This is a slightly different version of a question I asked you earlier in the book about challenge.

> Ask: What is something you have accomplished in your life that you are proud of?

Let your team tell stories of accomplishment. Then ask these questions:

- Did that accomplishment require risk?
- Did that accomplishment require you to embrace and utilize creative tension?

Ask the tribe members to share the risk and tension points that were critical to success. Discuss as a tribe a collective midair moment, from the past, you believe you navigated well and led to alchemy.

- How did the tribe navigate the midair moment?
- What helped the tribe stay through the tension points?
- What did the midair moment produce?

Relate the past midair moment to a current one. What can you learn from the past that can increase present success?

3. Learn in order to create better and better alchemy and celebrate to create camaraderie and energy for more alchemy.

Throw a Party, a Strategic and a Learning Oriented One

After your tribe has alchemized a challenge or opportunity, you need to throw a party. It can be a big party or a small one. The point is to celebrate. The party can last one minute, one hour, or one day. No matter the length or intensity, celebrating alchemy will heighten the achievement, no doubt. But there is another important, maybe more important, reason to celebrate. Celebrating alchemy increases the likelihood that you will embrace the process of alchemy, even the hard parts of the process, the next time it knocks on your tribe's door. The party also gives you a way to learn from your success (and failure) to enhance next iterations of alchemy.

In their book *Reframing Organizations* (2008), Lee Bolman and Terrence Deal suggest that celebrating helps "people let go of old attachments and embrace new ways of doing things" (p. 393). Have you ever thought about a celebration in that way? When celebrations get overly focused on partying about the outcomes (look what we accomplished), we don't celebrate that we were able to let go of the familiar, risk into creative space, engage the midair moment, and use collective skills in new ways (look how we *changed* in order to create alchemy).

Since you want these alchemy celebrations to reinforce the behaviors associated with alchemy, be strategic in your party throwing. Sure, it's fine to throw a party just because. But it's also important to strategically use celebrations to increase the quality and quantity of future alchemy. When you throw an alchemy party, try to bring these three gifts to it:

Gift One: As you celebrate, story-tell about the alchemy you've made, present and past.

Gift Two: As you celebrate, include moments in the celebrating that directly increase camaraderie.

Gift Three: As you celebrate, build the confidence of the tribe for future alchemy by learning together.

Gift One: Unwrap Storytelling about Alchemy, Present and Past

We all know that telling stories is essential to life. Stories help us make sense of life and identify with the various situations and relationships we encounter along the way. It seems that even neurobiology is getting in the storytelling game. Seems our brains even enjoy stories.

Paul J. Zak, professor at Claremont Graduate University and president of Ofactor, Inc., researched how storytelling affects the brain and produces oxytocin. In a October 28, 2014 *Harvard Business Review* digital article entitled "Why your Brain Loves Good Stories," Zak described what he did:

> To do this, we tested if narratives shot on video, rather than face-to-face interactions, would cause the brain to make oxytocin. By taking blood draws before and after the narrative, we found that character-driven stories do consistently cause oxytocin synthesis (n.p.)

What's powerful about this is that oxytocin is produced when we feel trusted or someone is kind to us.

Zak goes on to connect the stories a group tells to an increase in motivation and connection to their group. Zak especially connects this idea to organizations, but I would broaden it to all tribes (n.p.)

He continued in the digital article:

> My research has also shown that stories are useful inside organizations. We know that people are substantially more motivated by their organization's transcendent purpose (how it improves lives) than by its transactional purpose (how it sells goods and services).

Zak's point is easily transferable to alchemy. When people tell stories of alchemy during celebrations, it connects people to each other and to the work in ennobling ways. It enhances pride in the tribe, trust in the members, and energy for more alchemy. Telling the stories of alchemy should be like relating a good myth—with all the tensions and resolutions that go along with it.

Parties add another element to the storytelling. They are unique positive experiences that can turbocharge storytelling. Most of the time, but not always, parties elicit positive tribal mind-sets. Therefore, parties are a great time to tell tribal stories about the alchemy you are celebrating. Don't just celebrate that it's over. *Celebrate what happened to the tribe that led to alchemy.* Tell the story with dramatic enthusiasm and let other tribe members join in the retelling. Then the storytelling is not only fun to do, but it becomes strategic in that it helps you open the second and third gifts.

Gift Two: Unwrap an Increased *Camaraderie* for Future Alchemy

When your tribe tells the story of alchemy accomplished, get a number of tribe members involved in the telling. This often happens spontaneously. As members rehearse different parts of the alchemy story, they highlight important elements where they were involved or experienced something important along the way. There's a kind of handing off back and forth of the story between different tribe members that can occur during these moments. You want this back and forth to occur because it builds stronger bonds between tribe members and increases their camaraderie. People laugh, cry, get serious, or experience a host of other emotions as they share the telling of the story. I bet you oxytocin increases. Trust increases. Goodwill increases. And a desire to partner around alchemy also increases. The positive vibe strengthens resolve for the midair moments ahead.

Gift Three: Unwrap an Increased *Confidence* for Future Alchemy By Learning Together

As I mentioned, as different tribe members tell the story of alchemy, it builds goodwill and a positive vibe. But don't stop there. Don't let the moment go without also connecting the positive vibrations in the room to the *next rounds of alchemy needed to accomplish your tribe's mission.* This is where strategic use of the time and the story once again comes into play.

One of the best ways to be strategic at a party is to link the success of the past to the challenges and opportunities of the present and the future. Take the alchemy you're celebrating and use it to build the confidence of the tribe for what's ahead. Talk about current challenges and opportunities that you have not yet alchemized. Link to the success of the alchemy you are celebrating in order to build confidence for the next challenge or opportunity. Each one comes with its own unique situations that require the tribe to see, name, engage, and transform again. The alchemy gets better but it doesn't necessarily get easier to face the hard spots. This is something tribal leaders should do, no doubt. However, anyone in the tribe can and should speak in confidence-building ways that motivate the tribe toward its next challenge or opportunity.

If Eric Whitacre's first virtual choir video captured your attention, I suggest you now watch the third virtual choir video entitled, *Water Night*. Notice how the alchemy, the creativity, and the scope of the third virtual choir far outpaced the first one. This kind of iterative and progressive transformation happens when tribes celebrate *and* learn from past alchemy *and then* utilize their learnings and camaraderie in the future. Learning together then is not just about amassing knowledge, but about readying for the next situation where you will need collective ingenuity.

When you celebrate alchemy, recount different elements and circumstances that occurred in the magic making. But don't just talk about them with positive tones. Recount the circumstances and connect those circumstances to the risk and courage it took to meet the demands of those moments. Make the connection between the courage of the tribe and the outcome that courage produces. If you want to increase confidence, there's no time like a party to make the connection between demonstrated courage and desired outcomes. This moment of the party should be inspirational. Tribe members should be proud of their accomplishments and share in a healthy pride in their accomplishments.

SECTION FOUR:

Yes, There Is an "I" in Team:
Individual Member Practices That Make a Big Difference

The "I's" Matter

When I was growing up, there was a game in my house that I loved to play. It consisted of a round plastic plate, on top of which were approximately 15 individual plastic, bubble-like structures. A magnet, yellow on one side and black on the other, was inside each bubble structure. There was also a small plastic wand—maybe three or four inches long—with a magnet on one end. One side of the wand's magnet was black and the other was yellow.

The goal of the game was to place the wand on the bottom side of the plate where it would turn all the magnets to the color yellow or black. Sounds easy, right? Not exactly. The magnets did not act independently. So when I placed the wand under one of the individual magnets to turn it yellow, three others magnet would flip to their black sides. This created enormous frustration because just about the time you had all the magnets flipped to one color, a few would flip back to the other. I threw it across the room on several occasions. Luckily, or not, it was very sturdy.

After a few decades of working with tribes, the game from my childhood has become a powerful metaphor that highlights an essential dynamic: *individual tribe members affect each other in very specific and powerful ways.* It only takes one or two "out of sync" tribe members to flip many other tribe members upside down.

Thus far in the book I've emphasized the collective effort of groups to ingeniously use their raw materials to overcome challenges and seize opportunities. I would be remiss, however, if I did not highlight just how influential—for good or for ill—individual tribe members can be in the process of alchemy and the well-being of the tribe.

One, two, or ten (depending on the size of your tribe) misaligned tribe members with negative intentions can undo collective ingenuity and spread destructive attitudes. These attitudes and actions can overtake a tribe like a virus. I have witnessed individual tribe members wreak havoc through subtle and not so subtle sabotage. The force generated by their actions stalled innovation and deflated the energy required to make needed change. It is hard to overestimate the damage that can be done by such saboteurs. It is also sad when they are allowed to continue their ways because of ineffective leadership.

I have also witnessed the amazing energy and creativity individual tribe members can bring to a tribe because they are committed to their own self-development. I've watched as well-developed tribe members exude confidence in the midst of ambiguity and know-how in the midst of uncertain and difficult times. Not only are these types of tribe members magnetic and energizing, but they are often the starters and sustainers of the alchemy process.

No matter the tribe, leaders and engaged members alike want to populate their tribe with individuals who care about their own self-development and consistently pursue it with vigilance and intention. How individual tribe members behave in the pursuit of personal continuous improvement affects the well-being and creative productivity of the tribe. In other words, *when individual tribe members pursue personal excellence, rather than personal mediocrity, it increases the likelihood of tribal alchemy.* The oft-quoted phrase "There is no I in team" is both untrue and potentially very dangerous. There are many "I's" in tribes—and how each approaches his or her personal improvement—will affect the tribe.

The last brief section of this book explores *targeted practices* that tribe members can cultivate on a regular basis to ensure they are "alchemy-ready." Not only will these practices increase personal effectiveness, but they will also enable tribe members to lend their best energies to the alchemic process.

Here are the four practices (represented in the blue circle):

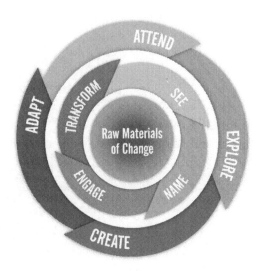

Attend: Pay attention to self, others, and situations.

Explore: Be curious and discovery-centered.

Create: Be creative in your life and work.

Adapt: Graciously flex with change.

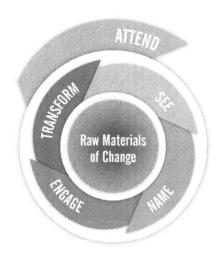

ALCHEMY-PRODUCING
TRIBE MEMBERS ATTEND

I thought it was a bad idea, but he insisted.

When my oldest son was around five years old, he did the "soccer thing." Early in the season, he became obsessed with the goalie position. On the way to every practice and game, it was all he could talk about. "Dad, I want to wear all the stuff the goalie gets to wear." I would sit in silence with a bit of a wince on my face. "Wouldn't that be great? Dad, wouldn't that be great?" he would repeat, with the same passion a child might gush for a chance to visit Willie Wonka's Chocolate Factory.

My lack of response to his desire came from my concern that the goalie position was not necessarily the best choice for him. He didn't have the most focused personality—he had a wanderlust at five that didn't seem to me to fit the job description of a goalie. My son's other obvious personality trait was his strong will. No matter how I tried to steer him toward a different position, he wouldn't budge. He wanted to be goalie, and that was that.

We made our way from our car to the field, where around 30 five-year-olds readied themselves for the match. Most parents chatted on the sidelines; some dreamed of retiring on the revenue of their kid's success; others maneuvered to ensure their child stood out and received pre-ferential treatment. I watched with some dread as Matt marched right up to his coach and made his case. At that point, fearing the worst, I constructed an apology in my mind to the coach and team. I would take the blame and throw myself under the bus for Matt. I could explain that I came from an athletically challenged gene pool—that sports just weren't our thing. I would promise to do better and quietly back Matt and myself into our car and slip away.

Matt got his way. He suited up and received instructions from his coach. For most of the first half Matt's team dominated—which seemed to please the dad next to me, who seemed one step away from asking the coach to put him in the game. Happily, the ball stayed pretty much down on the other side of the field. Though no scoring occurred, the other team didn't seem like much of a threat. I started to breathe easy.

Midway through the second half, one of the opposing team members stole the ball and kicked it hard. The ball rolled to midfield, where his teammate dribbled the ball and then kicked it toward the goal—toward Matt. Because the ball had never really made it to Matt's side of the field, no one was watching Matt. Our eyes had been focused on the other goal. In what seemed like a choreographed unison move, the entire crowd turned toward Matt (and the ball rolling toward his goal). As I made the turn, I heard a mom say, "Oh no, get up." At that point, everything went into slow motion (like that moment in a movie where someone is about to be shot, but then someone else tries to stop the shooter and normally ends up taking the bullet). There was Matt a few feet from the goal on all fours digging in the ground looking for buried treasure. Everyone was now shouting, "Get up, get up." The dad next to me reminded me of the angry version of the Incredible Hulk. I couldn't remember if he knew Matt was my son, but just for safety's sake I moved a few feet away. I mentally pulled out the apology and added a few more important lines about what my family *was* good at. As the opposing team's fan base cheered, Matt turned just in time to see the ball roll into the goal.

As we left the game that day, I reminded Matt that there were more games ahead. I also tried not to break into yet another lecture that had something to do with the fact that I had been against the whole "goalie thing" from the beginning. On the drive home, I reflected on how easy it was for me, indeed for all of us, to lose attention. Distractions and diversions abound in life. There are all sorts of shiny and even seemingly important things in the world that can keep us from attending.

There are limits, of course, to any one person's attention. We are unable to apply attention the way we would hope to in many situations. However, it is in the *act of attending* that we learn how to increase both the quality and frequency of our attention. Attending is a personal skill that yields personal benefits while simultaneously increasing one's ability to create alchemy with her tribe. Learning to attend with greater quality and more frequency comes as we take specific, conscious actions in moments of inattention. The actions:

1. Pausing
2. Noticing
3. Considering

When we combine these actions, we both diminish inattention and increase the ability to attend through moments of challenge and opportunity.

First, Pause

In the movie *Batman Begins*, Bruce Wayne learns to pay attention to himself (and his surroundings) by fighting his mentor, Ra's al Ghul. The sword fight takes place on a lake of frozen ice. During the fight, Ra's al Ghul activates Wayne's latent emotions of anger and fear through a series of volatile statements about the death of Wayne's parents. As the tension mounts, Wayne loses control of both his personal and situational awareness. In a move that Wayne believes establishes his dominance, he proudly directs Ra's al Ghul to yield as the loser. But Wayne's lack of awareness leaves him standing on thin ice, literally. A simple tap on the ice from Ra's al Ghul and Wayne falls through the ice into the freezing water below. His lack of attention led to dire consequences.

I've shown this clip to audiences for years. Once, when the sound went out while the clip rolled, I provided the dialogue myself. In other words, I know this clip inside and out. The more I watched it, over the years, the more I realized Wayne's demise occurred well before the ice breaks under his feet. As Ra's al Ghul's comments become more inflammatory, Wayne seems to rev up internally. The physical expression of this internal revving is flailing arms and mindless movements that leave him vulnerable to attack.

As the moment intensifies, his internal (and external) world speeds up, which is just the opposite of what is required to attend well in a moment. Though any given moment may be moving very fast, increasing our attention often requires that we bring a different pace to it rather than be swept along by its influence. The shift in pace often begins with a pause. Pausing, or *slowing* in a moment, enables the possibility of greater attention. The trick, of course, is to recognize your need to pause or slow before the moment is too far gone. This usually requires trial and error. We unfortunately have to fall through the ice—a number of times over a number of years—to learn how to attend better. And even after years of consistent success, we can still forget to pause, and fall right through again.

Learning to pause in the midst of a moment isn't just about a stop; it's about bringing a different quality of attention to the moment. Buddhists call this *mindfulness*. Jon Kabat Zinn, in his book *Wherever You Go, There You Are*, wrote, "Mindfulness means paying attention in a particular way: on purpose, in the present moment, and nonjudgmentally" (p. 4). We pause in order to remind ourselves that the moment is important enough to enter it more fully. When we pause, we gather up the better parts of ourselves in order to respond with wisdom. On the other hand, when we barge into a moment scattered and distracted, our inattention leads to mishaps; we fall through the ice.

The more mindful we are in our personal lives, the more we bring that gift to our tribes. During times of tribal ambiguity and stress, mindful members become promoters of calm. This allows for ingenious thought and action. None of us offers perfect mindfulness. We all lose mindfulness and need the support of others to re-center. The more we learn to pause and slow moments, the more we can bring awareness to any situation.

Then, Notice

In his novel *The Alchemist*, Paulo Cohelo tells the story of a young boy named Santiago. Santiago is on a journey to discover his Personal Legend. At one point, he is told a story of another young boy sent by his father out into the world to gain wisdom. The boy happens on a castle where a wise man lives. The wise man asks the boy to take a tour of his castle and its many intricacies and gardens. Before sending him on his way, he gives the boy a spoon with two drops of oil on it. The wise man instructs the boy to take in all the beauty of the castle and not allow the two drops of oil on the spoon to spill. Two hours later, the boy returns and the wise man asks him what he thought of all his marvels. The boy admitted to the man that he did not see the beauty of the castle because he was focused on keeping the oil on the spoon.

The wise man then sends the boy back out into his castle, with more oil on the spoon, into his castle and gardens. This time he exhorts the boy to take in all its wonders. The boy heeds the word of the man and is amazed at what he finds in the castle. When he returns, the wise man asks him where are the two drops of oil. The boy explains that he was so caught up by the wonders of the wise man's home that he didn't notice the oil had spilled off the spoon.

At this point the wise man says, "Well, there is only one piece of advice I can give you. The secret of happiness is to see all the marvels of the world, and never to forget the drops of oil on the spoon" (p. 32).

Noticing is what happens when we apply attention in a specific direction. It could be argued that noticing is the core of attending because it narrows attention onto an object or subject. With narrowed attention we can appreciate elements of the object or subject that were initially transparent to us. This is easy to illustrate.

Find an object near to you. It could be anything. First, pause to choose the thing that you will notice. Once you've chosen it, begin to notice it. Direct your attention to it in ways that open its various qualities to you. For example, I just noticed the white teacup sitting next to me has a reflection of my keyboard on it. Until I focused, the reflection appeared to be a color variation on the cup. But as I noticed, it became clear that the color variation was the reflection of my keyboard. Noticing this provided me an angle of view of my keyboard I've never had before.

When we focus our attention, we lose bandwidth but gain band "depth."

When I notice previously hidden qualities of an object or subject, it also increases the value of that object (not to mention the value of my noticing). This creates novelty, surprise, and a new strength of connection, and we go beyond awareness to appreciation. Appreciation then leads to the possibility of new ways of interacting.

In the documentary *The Pixar Story*, John Lassiter tells how research was done for the movie *A Bug's Life*:

> Research was literally done out in front of Pixar, in our own backyard. We ordered this tiny little video camera. We called it the bug cam and we put it on the end of a stick. We put little wheels from Lego on the bottom of it and we were able to wheel it around and literally look at things from a half inch above the ground. The one thing we noticed, from this bug cam, was how translucent everything was. It was breathtaking.

Notice that the focus on the Pixar grounds opened up a new view to Lassiter that had not been available to him in the past. This is what happens when we notice, specifically when we notice from different perspectives. Can you hear the Tribal Alchemy? This is why the personal cultivation of noticing is so important to Tribal Alchemy. If individuals within a tribe don't possess the skill of noticing, it will be unlikely they will see much of anything together.

Then, Consider

Considering adds a reflective quality to pausing and noticing. When we consider something, we stretch or extend it in a way that allows us to see it from different angles. This gives us the ability to take an idea, object, or relationship to a new or novel place. These new connections and possibilities form in the reflection, and that leads to creative expressions.

Again, consider this example from the Pixar documentary. Andrew Stanton, director of *Finding Nemo,* discussed the inspiration for the movie:

> I remember in '92, when my son was just born, we went to Marine World . . . and they had this shark exhibit. You kind of walked through a tunnel and they swim over you . . . it was like a glass tunnel. You could get up really close, see underwater, and lose all your peripheral vision and anybody around you in the man-made world. And I remember thinking then, you know we could make this world. CG would be perfect for this world . . . it would capture it so well.

When we add "considering" to attending and noticing, we allow curiosity to guide us into new possibilities. We link seemingly separate ideas into new combinations that lead to the possibility of alchemy. There is, of course, a personal alchemy that is also essential to living well. And when we have reflective awareness, we are more likely to see new ways to use what we have to create what we need.

Ways to *consider* more regularly:

1. Ask questions that open up new ideas rather than highlighting already confirmed ones.
2. Make connections between seemingly random events or objects.
3. Have connection-making conversations with others. Pay attention to the connections other people make.
4. Notice the interconnection of objects and events that were previously disconnected for you. For example, take a piece of

fruit or a vegetable. Place it in front of you and think about what it took, all the connections that had to be made, in order for you to have that food. Once you've moved beyond the obvious ones, try to think of four or five more. You will be amazed at the connections you find.

5. Add reflection time to experiences. After watching a movie or engaging in an activity, spend a few minutes reflecting on the experience and how it affected you.

. . .

If individual tribe members don't attend well, how will tribal alchemy suffer?

- The ability to see (together) is diminished.
- Tribal members miss or diminish important but differing perspectives.
- The "POP" goes unnoticed (the tribe yawns in front of the creative solution).
- Opportunities are overlooked.
- Challenges breed perpetual complaining.
- Tribal members miss each other's cues for support and encouragement.
- Camaraderie wanes.
- Circling and reflecting are replaced with territorialism and individual agendas.
- Collective mind is lost.
- Collective intelligence wanes.
- Collaboration is reduced to individuals doing things together.
- There is more "telling" and less inquiry.
- Questions are laced with personal agendas.

ALCHEMY-PRODUCING
TRIBE MEMBERS EXPLORE

I suppose my boys were around seven and nine years of age at the time. It was summer, and, as always, they enjoyed the long and lazy days with friends. One of their favorite activities that summer was to ride bikes in the mud. If there was mud anywhere nearby, my boys and their friends could find it. Consequently, they developed a bad habit of using the hose to wash off their bikes. In and of itself this was not a problem, that is, until they would leave the hose on, for, oh, an hour—or worse, use it to create a mud pit on the side of the house.

"Guys, I don't want you to use the hose anymore this summer. You can brush the mud off your bikes once it has dried. Got it?" The edict came down with a good bit of intensity, and I was sure the message had been received. So you can imagine my chagrin when, the next day, I heard the familiar sound of water outside the house. I took a quick peek out the window only to see my boys back in the business of bike cleaning with the hose. All their friends gathered around and laughed as they sprayed their tires. My parental prowess had evaporated in less than 24 hours.

"This situation requires my 'Dad tone,'" I thought to myself. Translation: It's time to act like a jerk—not a big jerk, mind you, just a little one—and coerce my boys into a new behavioral pattern. I flung the screen door open and with the Dad tone said, "Hey guys, what's up? Don't you remember what we talked about yesterday?" All the other boys tried to muffle their laughter as I approached and launched into my jerky behavior. "I told you not to use the hose."

"But Dad," my seven-year-old jumped in, "you don't understand."
I kneeled down, "No, I understand. It's you two that don't understand."

As I stood there, I noticed the water as it dripped off the wheels of my youngest son's bike. And then I saw the mud. It was caked in between the knobs of his motocross tires. "Guys, look. Just wipe this off with your hands; it's not going to kill you." I demonstrated the procedure with my hands as more muted tones of laughter came my way. Now I was mad. There was something wrong with this picture.

"But Dad," my youngest son pleaded as he laughed.

"No Andrew, I don't want to hear the excuses—now turn the hose off and come help me."

"Dad," he protested with greater intensity, as I continued to clean off the tires.

"What, Andrew, what is it?" I barked.

"Um . . . that's not mud you're cleaning off." Snickers ensued. "Um . . . well . . . Dad, that's dog poop."

At that point, it did cross my mind to declare that I had known all along it was dog poop. But I figured it wouldn't be good to add lying to the moment—I already had the mild jerk thing going. I smiled, and then the laughter erupted. My youngest simply smiled and handed me the hose. I asked him to turn it on full blast.

I wonder what might have been different if I had explored
rather than declared.

Most people stop looking when they find the proverbial needle in the haystack. I would continue looking to see if there were other needles.
Einstein

He who thinks he is finished, is.
Jewish Proverb

The trouble with know-it-alls is that they are so irritating.
The trouble with know-it-alls is they are so rigid.
The trouble with know-it-alls is that they are arrogant.
The trouble with know-it-alls is that they are wrong, because they don't-know it all.
There's always trouble when I'm a know-it-all.

The second practice invites us to live discovery-based lives. It's easy to become overly comfortable with our knowledge and experience. We can stop exploring because of fear, apathy, incompetence, or overconfidence, to name a few. To live the life of an explorer is to maintain what Buddhists call "a beginner's mind." This means we remain free of rigid expectations, preconceptions, and unhealthy judgments. We remain open to new ideas even if they challenge our cherished beliefs and knowledge.

I have coached a number of gifted leaders (some with formal positional power and some with informal influence). One common denominator that separates the exceptional leader from the adequate one is that the exceptional leader understands that she has much more to learn and explore. The adequate, not to mention the irritating, leaders all seem to believe they have achieved a knowledge or stature that justifies a dismissive and sometimes even arrogant posture.

When we have a lack of curiosity or desire to explore, we limit our tribe's alchemic reach. As we've seen, alchemy requires a willingness to move beyond *what is* and explore *what could be*. We know that individuals within a tribe influence the alchemy process. Therefore, if tribe members, for whatever reason, are unwilling to explore new perspectives, the tribe collectively suffers. This is why it's important for individual tribe members to cultivate their own sense of discovery and possibility-oriented thinking and living.

Perhaps the first step in becoming a more curious and discovery-oriented individual is to locate areas of life where we are acting *as if* we already know it all. Few of us would actually declare that we know everything there is to know about a given subject or circumstance, so we have to look at behaviors. Being a know-it-all begins when we are unwilling to shift behavior (and belief) because of an inflated sense of "rightness." Because I entered the "mud on the tire moment" with fixed expectations, I was not willing to explore other possibilities. I already had it all figured out and didn't need any further information or insight. In fact, when faced with the invitation to explore beyond my own conception, I became defensive and dismissive. These are sure signs of a curiosity deficit.

The question then becomes, what can we do to reduce know-it-all behaviors and increase a beginner's mind?

Shifting

We shift.

You see it all the time.

We sit too long in one position, it gets uncomfortable, and so we shift. Every day we live out patterns that create meaning. We get up, we go to work or school or wherever it is we go. We eat, we talk, we laugh, we consume—and on it goes. These routines are important because they create bonds that provide life a kind of stability. However, there is a potential danger that awaits us in these daily patterns. If we settle into patterns in a way that makes us too comfortable, if we don't change them up from time to time, we will grow numb—just like our leg, foot, or arm falls asleep if it's in the same position for too long.

When we go numb to life, we lose a sense of wonder and curiosity. Days become like objects on an assembly line, passing us in succession as we apply the same thoughts and actions to each one. The patterns themselves are not necessarily negative and may help us make sense of life. But if we don't regularly move beyond those patterns they become hazards rather than helpful boundaries.

Shifting out of our predictable patterns opens us to novel experiences that challenge our understanding of the world and open us to new ways of seeing it. Curiosity is a practice that helps us shift our attention and wake up to the possibility of "the more," or "the unexpected." Curiosity is also a quality of attention that allows us to experience a refreshed meaning in familiar places. Curiosity keeps exploring.

In order to shift to curiosity, we have to first notice when our life patterns have put us to sleep. Numbness to life can take many forms: apathy, lethargy, pervasive sarcasm, or overindulgence, to name a few. Reading our moods and actions can be a clue. Listening to those we trust—if they see numbness overtaking us—can also be helpful, though it can be difficult to hear them if we are numb. At these times, feedback can leave us defensive or reactive, or both, which can also be signs of numbness. Whether internal or external, a regular evaluation of our behavior can reveal needed shifts.

Willingness to take stock, as well as move out of rigidity, requires we add another element to the mix that can make it easier to shift: *discontentedness*.

Get Discontent

When we are discontent, it either leads to apathy (of some sort) or curiosity. The choice is ours.

> Is it good to be content?
> It depends.
> I want to rush out and buy the newest Mac product. Mine is still working just fine. I suppose it's good to be content—for now.

Is it good to be content?

It depends.

I'm stuck in a job I hate. I know I should make a change, and I'm making everyone around me miserable. I suppose it would be good to be discontent and curious about what is "possible."

Is it good to be content?

It depends.

I have a 150 cable channels. Will 300 make my life richer and more full of meaning? Perhaps being content is a good idea.

Is it good to be content?

It depends.

I'm in a relationship that is destructive, but won't do anything about it. Maybe it's time to get discontent.

It's a tricky moment when we are discontent. Sometimes it's helpful and sometimes it's not. Learning which kind of disconnectedness you're experiencing takes practice, failure, guidance, and patience.

Remember, if you think you're finished, you are.

There is a kind of discontent that is good. This discontent can be as simple as the discontent about the route you take to work or any other pattern in your life. The discontent that leads to curiosity is the feeling of being sick and tired of being sick and tired and requires a willingness to explore changes and new possibilities. One day, over 20 years ago, I got tired of being sick and overweight. I got curious about what I could do to change my body. Now, more than two decades later, I'm still 40 or more pounds lighter and in the best shape of my life. I did this because I became discontent about "what was" and curious about "what could be."

I'm not suggesting that you should be discontent about everything that is not exciting and new. Changing jobs, relationships, or anything else you can think of is not necessarily the answer. I would never suggest to anyone that, at the first sign of discontent, you change your world for a new one. We know that changing our external world may create a temporary newness that can be exciting but eventually leads us right back to a dysfunction we were not initially willing to face.

Getting discontent, in order to explore, isn't always about replacing what we have. It's about a new way to see what is and wonder about what it could become. Making significant life changes, because of discontentedness, should be done with thoughtfulness and the wisdom of trusted friends and advisors. Often it's the neglect of what we have that is the problem to overcome. Sometimes our curiosity should lead us to renew what we have, to make alchemy with what we have, rather than looking for something else. Herein lies one of the most challenging aspects of life and exploration: when is it time to move on and when is it time to renew what we have? Either way, discontentedness is a necessary part of the exploration.

Explorers are discontent.

Venture Out

The antidote for discontentedness comes when we venture out. When we venture out, we summon the power of curiosity and aim it at a particular intention.

I wonder

I wonder what

I wonder what would happen

I wonder what would happen if

What if?

How does?

Where are?

Venturing out begins with fresh questions. What questions do you need to ask?

Curiosity is fueled by questions, and questions are fueled by curiosity. Statements do of course have a place in life, but they can reduce the wonder of life if we're not careful. Of course declarations can be powerful when they open us to the power inside us. Declarations are stifling, however, when they close down creative exploration. For example:

- That'll never work.
- I've already tried that.
- Things will never change.
- It's all my fault.
- It's all your fault.

A well-designed question is often the beginning of a new venture.

Questions create possibilities because they open us to what we don't know, what is beyond us and what might happen if we altered our approach. *Questions are the carriers of curiosity*. Become a world-class question maker and venture out.

Venturing out into new mind-sets and actions requires we add risk to our questioning.

We've already explored the concept of risk, the midair moment. As much as risk is necessary for a tribe, it is equally necessary that individuals learn the power and practice of risk. Everything we explored earlier about the midair moment is applicable to you as an individual.

Risk activates an energy that allows the venturing out to occur. When I teach on risk, I will often ask an audience to think of a personal accomplishment that makes them proud. I then ask people to raise their hands if they were able to achieve that accomplishment without any risk. Of course, I've never had one person raise their hand. Significant accomplishments require risk. When we learn to navigate personal midair moments, we are able to bring that skill to the tribe when it faces the risks inherent in challenges and opportunities.

Stay Humble

When we are appropriately discontent, when we venture out and ask questions, we are demonstrating humility. Know-it-alls aren't discontent—except with everyone else. They don't venture out; they expect others to come to them. And they declare far more often than they ask. Humility, on the other hand, grounds a person in the reality that they have much to learn and therefore need humility.

Humility grounds me to two realities:

- I am finite and frail and there is so much to life than I can't fathom.
- I have ability to search out the unknown and unexplored territory.

The word *humble* has partial origins in the Latin word *humus*, which literally meant "on the ground." Humility then *isn't* about having an ever-diminishing view of yourself. It's about having an appropriate and grounded view that allows you to explore with wisdom. Searching the unknown and unexplored requires humility because without it, we might barge into situations that leave us, and others, vulnerable to unnecessary danger.

Mapmakers used to draw pictures of dragons at the edge of the known world. "Here be dragons" was the warning. This warning should certainly engender humility when venturing beyond the known territory. Humble venturing is an action we all need to develop when encountering the unknown. *Humility doesn't eliminate a confident search of "what could be"; it enables it.* Neither is humility fear based. Some might look at the dragons and shrink back out of fear. Humility allows us to enter the unknown with healthy apprehension. Healthy apprehension helps us move at the right pace and intensity so that our venturing out has the best chance of leading to new discoveries rather than new dysfunctions.

. . .

If individual tribe members don't explore well, how will Tribal Alchemy suffer?

- Arrogance overrides a humble search for "the better."
- Important opportunities and challenges go unnamed and are framed in negative ways.
- Creative tension is sacrificed for predictable and comfortable behaviors.

- Learning is devalued.
- Easy answers eclipse new solutions.
- Curiosity is punished.
- Group think settles in.
- Excuses douse possibilities.
- Viewpoints are defended rather than expanded.
- Energy wanes.
- Rigidity increases.
- New territory goes unmapped.

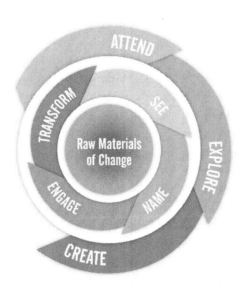

ALCHEMY-PRODUCING TRIBE MEMBERS CULTIVATE CREATIVITY

A number of years ago a friend asked me to speak to her college art class about artful living. The college was located in downtown Pittsburgh, Pennsylvania. I arrived early—which seems to be a dysfunction of mine—and decided to walk around the streets of the city. At one point I noticed a cluster of tents and a crowd of people gathered. Curiosity got the better of me, and I moved toward the action.

What I found was a group of international ice sculptors in town for a competition. For the next half hour, I was mesmerized even though every extremity of my body protested the cold temperature. I had to stay and watch. With chainsaws and a plethora of picks and chisels, these arctic artisans created frozen statues of hockey players, cartoon characters, and whatever else you could imagine.

Inside the classroom I found a group of college freshmen who dared me to engage them. I shared my experience with the ice sculptors. I relayed that most of the artists had nothing more than a simple scribbled picture from which to work. I demonstrated the movement the artists made—moving from the picture to the ice, back to the picture, and then back to the ice.

I continued, "How do you think they get the ice to look like the picture? There's no template to put on the ice. They don't outline the ice. They simply look at the picture and put their instruments on the ice. Something occurs between their glance at the picture and their action on the ice. Something invisible becomes tangible. What do you think that invisible "something" is?" At this point three students were asleep, two were drooling, and the rest looked like the proverbial deer in headlights. Eventually, though, they got it, and our discussion took off.

For the next hour we talked about that "something" and named it *creative action*.

My winter-day encounter with ice sculptors reminded me that *creating* happens when we apply both skill and a certain kind of mindfulness to whatever it is we are doing. When we are creative individuals, we bring to our tribes our personal ability to transform raw materials into something better. Once again, when we make alchemy (create) in our personal lives, it makes us better at the tribal variety as well. Tribes ought to encourage their members to explore personal creativity if for no other reason than the positive effect it will have on tribal alchemy.

When we create, just like the sculptor, we bring something into existence through action. *What* we create doesn't have to be as complex as an ice sculpture. We can create a meal, a good conversation, an exercise routine, a poem, a painting, or just a simple gift for a friend (and more). Creating shouldn't be just about what we produce (although we will see that too is important) but about the cultivation of mind-sets and actions that enable creative expression. When we cultivate those mind-sets and actions, we enrich our own lives and enhance our effectiveness as a tribe member.

Entire books, many of them, explore the process of creativity. In the next few sections, I simply want to highlight four elements that increase personal creativity and ready you to contribute to tribal alchemy as well.

I saw these four elements of creativity that day in chilly Pittsburgh:

- Creativity requires space and time.
- Originality and creativity are linked.
- Creativity enables us to make stuff (and moments).
- Share what you make.

Creativity Requires Space and Time

The first dynamic the ice sculptors revealed about creativity is that it requires *space and time*. We have to make a room for it. Sometimes this means reserving hours in the day and space in our environment to make something creative. This could be a painting, a musical piece, a floral arrangement, or a thousand other possibilities. We tend to think of these creations as artistic expressions, and for good reason. But of course there are numerous daily activities, not normally thought of as art, that can still be done with creativity.

In a sense everyday moments can become art if done with creativity. A great conversation, a walk on the beach, a meeting at work, time spent with family, and a variety of other everyday activities can be creative acts—if, that is, we avoid the mindless approaches that often overtake our daily routines. Making room for creativity, then, is sometimes about dedicated time and space to make something. At other times, though, it's simply about the insertion of a creative spirit *into* daily routines. Either way, what we must first do is make room for creativity. Until we do that, creativity lies dormant like a barren field in winter.

We make room for creativity in many ways. But there is a 21st-century obstacle to overcome if we want to make room for creativity. We must step off the unending, unsatisfying *road of busyness*.

Stepping Off the Road of Busyness

In my late twenties, I spent a little over a year living in southern Maryland, near Washington DC. I worked at a counseling center three days a week. As is often the case, I had breaks in between appointments, sometimes up to two or three hours. Because the counseling center was quite a distance from my home, I often spent those breaks at local parks.

I grew up in Phoenix, Arizona, where a park was a plot of ground with some swings and a basketball court. I was therefore blown away the first time I went to a mid-Atlantic state park. To me, it was like entering a forest. A walk in one of these parks often became the highlight of my day.

One day, I noticed a community garden where people living nearby could rent space to grow fruits and vegetables. This was also a new concept to me—renting space for a garden. I was intrigued. But what intrigued me even more was that no matter what time of day I passed the gardens, I only saw elderly people attending to the growth. Of course I understand that many people were probably at work and/or taking care of their families during daytime hours. I'm also sure there were younger people who also had gardens. However, my observation revealed an unfortunate reality about life. People often make more space and time for creativity after they've retired or as they enter into the last season of life. This does make sense to some degree because earlier in life many demands and obligations assail us from every direction. We don't have as much time and space. However, this also becomes an excuse by which we justify not making any time or space for things that would enable creativity, not to mention general health and wellbeing.

Busyness is a favorite justification that keeps us from creativity. We are simply too busy to spend any time on nonessential activity. And nonessential activity often includes space and time for creative endeavors, not to mention simply living a more mindful life. Many people wear busyness as a badge of honor. When you ask them how they're doing, without hesitation, they answer that they are "busy" with no relief in sight. Unfortunately, busyness is mostly a convenient way to avoid behaviors and activities that either we don't like or are difficult to do. It is initially much easier to sit on the couch and watch television than it is to enter into a more creative act. It may also be initially easier to "busy ourselves" with unnecessary work in order to avoid creative action that could make a real difference. Some have suggested that busyness is a form of laziness. I tend to agree.

Even when we are in seasons of life that demand a lot of attention and energy—because of our circumstances—we can still make time for creative expressions. And we can certainly infuse more creativity and mindfulness into the everyday activities that occupy us. The question is: Am I willing to devote even small amounts of time to more creative action?

It's hard to talk about other elements of creativity if we have not first made space and time for them. Making personal space and time for creative acts also allows us to be comfortable with the necessary space and time required to make Tribal Alchemy. Too often, tribe members who are personally busy derail alchemy because they hurry the tribe to a conclusion before the alchemy is discovered. Hurrying to a premature conclusion—as a tribe—is often the result of people being unwilling to give a challenge or opportunity the space and time it needs to unfold, not to mention the space and time the tribe needs to find the alchemy.

Eliminating busyness doesn't mean that we will sit around with nothing to do or in constant unproductiveness. On the contrary, it means that we focus on those essential activities and relationships that make life richer. It also means we have the internal and external space and time to bring to those activities and relationships our more creative self. Then life, and its varied situations and circumstances, becomes a block of ice waiting for us to add shape and texture. Are you making space and time to be creative?

Originality and Creativity are Linked

When I was a freshman in high school, I fell into a little hero worship of a senior named Steve. To me, Steve pretty much walked on water—he could do no wrong. He became an icon of coolness; a short ninth grader could only hope to someday be in a similar zip code of cool. Steve exuded confidence. He was popular. He was a musician, excelled in academics, and dated pretty much whomever he wanted. You get the picture.

As an impressionable freshman, I was looking for role models. Steve was number one on my list. Over time, I was bold enough to actually strike up a conversation with Steve, and he actually seemed to like me. We became casual friends. As I hung out with Steve, I found myself trying hard to be like him. There was just one problem: I wasn't Steve.

Steve had wavy hair that fell in tiny, circular wisps all over his head. My hair was as straight as the street I grew up on, and when freshly cut, it struck straight out of my head. Steve was lean and about 5' 11" inches tall. My freshman year, a teacher mistook me for a student who had wandered across the street from the elementary school. Let's just say I was barely 4' 11" tall. I was a short, slightly overweight runt—if you can imagine that combination.

I could go on, but you get the idea. As a freshman, it was hard for me to be okay with myself because—well, there was Steve. He was a living reminder of everything I wanted to be. Because of my desire to be like Steve, it became hard to find my own life and my own voice. This icon overshadowed me, and for a small bit of time I gave up my own life in pursuit of his. Luckily for me, he graduated, which forced me to continue my own growth.

. . .

Each ice sculptor had his or her own original style. This made each sculptor's creation unique, with the fingerprint of the sculptor all over the art. Roaming around that winter day, I could see the different stylistic approaches each artist brought to his or her work. This is true for all art forms. Artists become known for their unique expressions, whether in music, dance, painting, or any other artistic medium. The same is true for everyday expressions of creativity. People become known for adding their particular flair to a situation or relationship. When describing the behavior of a person to another, the other person might say something like, "That is so Dave." This phrase means that the actions of "Dave" reflected his personality, strengths, and/or weakness. In other words, Dave's actions revealed his originality.

When we are most ourselves we are most original.

May Sarton, a 20th-century American poet and novelist, wrote a poem with an intriguing title. She named it, "Now I Become Myself." Here are the first four lines:

> Now I become myself. It's taken
>
> Time, many years and places;
>
> I have been dissolved and shaken,
>
> Worn other people's faces.

It's true, isn't it? We try on many faces before settling on our own. Being authentic and original is a lifelong endeavor with many twists and turns. But it's worth the effort. It allows us to experience and express something unique in the world. Not only is that personally rewarding, but it's also valuable for our tribes. Tribes benefit from the originality of their members because it creates a rich diversity of vision and action. As we explored earlier, embracing and layering the different (original) perspectives and skills of tribe members, though difficult at times, is essential for great alchemy.

Creativity Enables Us to Make Stuff (and Moments)

Creativity needs a home. It doesn't have to be a fancy home or an expensive one. But creativity eventually must lead to the production or enhancement of something, someplace, or someone. What is powerful about what we make is not just that it exists (though that alone is amazing) but that it becomes an ongoing reminder of the power and process of creativity. This also means that the more we can look at our everyday lives as a series of creative actions that lead to creative moments, objects or relationships, the more meaningful our lives will become. Then we can supply our tribes with that same kind of transformative power.

If you want to be creative, you've got to make stuff. "Stuff" can be tangible or intangible. There are creative ideas (intangible) and creative objects (tangible). The commonality between them is the creativity that led to their existence. Look around you and try and identify things you've created. Are there any objects you have made or alchemized lately? Then think back over the past week and ask yourself how many times during the week did you infuse time and space with creativity? Collect those moments as you would collect treasures at a craft fair, because they represent creativity in action.

I'm convinced life would be more meaningful if we would collect more moments and objects that we've created. When we hold these moments and objects in a portfolio of creativity, they become markers of the life we want to experience and express on an ongoing basis. Imagine you could hang a moment like you hang a painting. What if you could keep everyday creative action like you keep music or poems? Perhaps this is why some people write journals. It provides a way to capture creative moments so they are accessible in the future.

What have you created lately? Can you point to it or describe it? At the end of the ice sculptor completion, each artist had a piece of work that reveled his creative effort. If you and I are creative, both in the traditional sense and in the everyday sense, we should be able to point to creative works that are the result of our effort.

Share What You Make

The ice sculptors seemed happy to share their art, many of them doing so as they were creating. They talked to each other and to the assembled crowd. There was something important that occurred because they shared their art during and after its creation. That "something" has to do with community. Creative expressions bring people together, not only to appreciate the art, but also to appreciate shared passions that inspire and energize. This is often how tribes form in the first place. They gather around shared creativity and/or passion to make or do something specific in the world.

There is no doubt that creative expressions are meaningful even if the creator is the only who experiences them. However, what is made is meant to be shared. Human connection and enrichment happens in the sharing that completes the circle, if you will. This is why it's important for a receiver to confirm to the creator that he "sees" what has been made. And it's also why its important for the creator to share what she has made. It seems that "show and tell" is not just for kids at school. We all have a desire to share because it validates the energy it took to be creative, and it connects us with like-minded people.

My suggestion is that friends or tribe members have "show and tell parties." Meet up and talk about what you've all created lately. If it's an object, then bring it. If it's an intangible, then talk about it. Don't worry about how good the art is; focus on sharing the process of creativity that enabled you to create it. You could also talk about what you might do more or less of next time in order to enhance it.

There is also something powerful about putting ourselves out there and sharing our creations with others. It's a good risk that may not always yield the responses we want, but it will always give us the opportunity to put our voice or "art" out there to inspire and serve others. This risk of revealing creativity comes in handy when your tribe must risk its way into alchemy. There are times when you, as an individual, will be the catalyst to move alchemy forward. This can be a risky moment. Once again, it will require you to put yourself out there without knowing how people will respond to your overtures and ideas. Learning to humbly yet confidently share your creativity—in a safe environment—can help you share your ideas and skills with your tribe during a challenge or opportunity.

. . .

If individual tribe members don't create well, how will tribal alchemy suffer?

- Alchemy is replaced with mediocrity.
- Energy wanes due to a lack of risk.
- The tribe is eclipsed by the innovations of other tribes.
- Yesterday's success is "good enough."
- Unproductive diversions eclipse appropriate urgency.
- Ingenuity is replaced with inflexible control.
- Invention hides its secrets.
- Artistry is suppressed.
- Failure is quietly forbidden.
- Boundaries shrink.
- Action is void of meaning.

- Apathy and lethargy emerge.
- Greatness is downplayed or altogether missed.
- Accomplishment breeds jealousy.

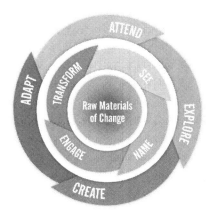

ALCHEMY-PRODUCING TRIBE MEMBERS GRACIOUSLY FLEX

I love guacamole and salsa. Actually, that is an understatement of significant proportions. The unfortunate part of this love affair is that the "dipping tool" of choice for both guacamole and salsa is usually deep fried, overly salted and completely addicting. Yep. Chips. I avoid chips these days in order to eat "clean" and remain a happy person. "Overweight Dave" is grumpy. Of course, when you love something, you find ways around the tough spots in order to spend time with the object of your desire. My solution to my dipping dilemma is veggies. Carrots, cucumbers, celery and peppers are great replacements for chips. If I could only convince restaurants of this fact. I guess the simplest way to describe my problem is that I have an ongoing tug-of-war with restaurant servers about veggies for dipping.

It would seem that replacing chips with veggies should be no big deal. Now, I know if a restaurant doesn't have veggies, they won't be able to serve them. Or if the kitchen alchemists are extremely busy, they may not have time to cut veggies. I understand all of this, I really do. The ongoing saga begins before the request goes to the kitchen. My veggie dilemma starts with a conversation with servers about the *possibility* of replacing chips with veggies. To be fair, occasionally I get a server who understands the request and simply says, "Yes, we can do that," or, "No, we can't." Most of the time, though, my request sends servers into something between irritation and panic. I've watched servers freeze with uncertainty as if I had asked them to solve the mystery of dark energy. I've had servers get irritated with me as if I were asking them to run down the street, order me food from a different restaurant, bring it back and personally feed it to me. It seems this whole veggie-replacing-chip thing is a lesson in adaptability.

My ongoing guacamole-salsa saga reminds me of our tendency, as human beings, to become rigid. Servers become rigid about the special orders. Chefs become rigid about preparation. I become rigid about their rigidity. It's hard to adapt. Servers, chefs, and I don't want to adapt. And when one of those three parties (servers, chefs, Dave) does adapt, it's often not a very graceful adaptation. Though we may know it's usually a good thing, adapting can be hard; particularly when the adaptation requires us to move into uncomfortable places (embracing the unfamiliar or releasing the known).

As we explored early in the book, human beings seek to conserve energy and find equilibrium just as soon as we lose comfort and security. We do this in order to feel safe, or to face threats. When it comes to survival in harsh and dangerous conditions, this strategy makes sense. If I'm lost in the forest and low on food, it's not time to do an hour's worth of exercise. The trouble is that our brains don't immediately know the difference between the threat of say, a wild animal chasing us down the street, and the threat of a change within our tribe that causes uneasiness. When we feel threatened—in the midst of challenge or opportunity—we can easily become rigid and graceless. This lack of pliability and openness to others can make us personal obstacles to Tribal Alchemy, and, generally speaking, a pain in the butt of the tribe.

When it comes to the accomplishment of a mission, remaining rigid and obstinate is a liability that has implications for us as individuals as well as for the entire tribe. It's not that strategies to achieve security and safety should be avoided at all costs, but rather *when and how* we employ them during times of tribal challenge and opportunity. Adaptive action begins when we *graciously flex with needed change.* This description highlights two important elements to adaptive behavior: (1) the need for a gracious attitude, and (2) the need for resilience and pliability in the midst of change. Let's take a look at both.

A Gracious Attitude

I'm a morning person. When we think of "morning" people, we tend to think of the cheery greeting first thing in the morning from a person who pops out of bed ready to go. This in fact may be the case and does to some degree describe me. But being a morning person also means that I exhibit a predictable set of nighttime behaviors. "Cheery" and "ready to go" would not be good descriptors of my nighttime behaviors. And unless I'm standing up in front of people speaking or leading a meeting, my nighttime behaviors begin between 8:00 and 9:00 p.m. And yes, just to cut to the chase, I've fallen asleep during dinner parties, family gatherings, movies, deep conversations, and parties, to name a few. I also have the ability to fall asleep within minutes, sometimes seconds, of feeling tired. Friends and family all have their stories of experiencing what I call, "the light switch." One second I'm talking to you, and the next I'm asleep. There is absolutely no exaggeration in that description.

Knowing my proclivity for early evening dozing will help you appreciate why a lovely dinner, highly anticipated by my wife and I, went so bad.

We had been at the dinner table for three hours. Now, let's just stop right there. Three hours! My family of origin ate dinner in 15 minutes and had the dishes done and put away 15 minutes after that. Yes, as an adult, I've learned the art of "staying longer" at tables and parties, but three hours is pushing it on my best days. Oh, and by the way, it was also after 8:00 p.m. In fact, dinner started at 7:30. I like eating a late dinner. It makes me feel like a savvy European. But "cheery" and "ready to go" do not describe me after 8:00 p.m., not to mention the fact that my tablemates were all far more extroverted than I, the restaurant was loud, and the conversation was rapid fire with few breaks in between.

As we moved well beyond 8:00 p.m., I felt the usual emotional and bodily signals overtake me. My eyes started to get heavy and I began hallucinating. I think there was a bed or couch in my vision. My body moved into hibernation mode. I experienced the predictable unhappiness about everything—and everyone—that is blocking me from a comfortable and flat surface. In other words, my attitude went down very fast as the night wore on—particularly since everyone else seemed, well, happy.

Just a few minutes after leaving the restaurant, I found myself angry, tired, and looking for a place to deposit my frustration. This, of course, is what family members are for. My wife endured the brunt of my tirade against loud restaurants, fast-talking people, and long evenings. Somehow it was her fault for all of these variables, and I wanted to make sure she appreciated the compromising position she'd so willfully put me in. She was a convenient runway on which to land my own discomfort and foul mood. Of course, it did not ease anything, as you can imagine.

The brain and activation point

The study of neurobiology regularly reveals more secrets of the brain and how behavior is linked to the function of the brain. Of course with every mystery solved, three more emerge that confound scientists. These new mysteries keep alive the search for more understanding. What is also humbling about this pursuit is that new discoveries often undo past ones. Remember the left-brain/right-brain craze? We now know that idea was overblown, as was the idea that we only use 10% of our brains. When it comes to understanding how our "wiring" affects our behavior, we have a long way to go to understand its mysteries.

What does seem clear, and is confirmed by much evidence, is that when we feel insecure or threatened, for whatever the reason, we respond from older parts of the brain that focus on survival and safety. We know this as the fight-or-flight response. This fight-or-flight response is now understood to include freeze and flock as other primal responses to perceived danger.

What's also clear is that when we are feeling vulnerable or threatened, we have a diminished ability to remain gracious toward others and ourselves. This diminished capacity for graciousness has ramifications for tribes that go unspoken or misspoken (as when tribe members talk about the graceless behavior of other tribe members when they are not present). When a tribe member is activated biologically and emotionally, his or her lack of graciousness can quickly zap the energy from other tribe members. Tribes can ride the moods of certain individuals like a roller coaster at Disney World. In fact, tribe members often have signaling systems and phrases they use to alert each other of graceless attitudes. "Stay away from Dave. He's in one of his moods." "Red alert, she's at it again." "Avoid Tom, enough said." Sometimes these signaling systems are nonverbal, consisting of eye rolls, head shakes, or gesticulations.

When a tribe member is graceless due to vulnerability, it's a tricky moment. The attitude can do damage to a tribe's ability to alchemize. Yet the affected (or infected) tribe member may not be able to "just stop" his behavior. We know that once we are triggered, we make less enlightened decisions, and it takes some time to reestablish higher level reflection and action. Can we mitigate our dysfunctional moods when we are emotionally activated? That answer depends on a host of variables that influence us during times of emotional activation. These include diet, sleep, a host of situational factors, including our level of mindfulness about the trigger and the current situation. With all this in mind, remaining gracious during times of vulnerability requires consistent practice and personal strategies for identifying and navigating these moments from a place of greater awareness. And that is much easier said than done. If we have any hope of diminishing the effect of our activation, it will be because we understand what triggers us and what we can do about those triggers. Identifying, noticing and mindfully navigating triggers is often the first element of becoming a more adaptable person.

Know the Triggers That Make You Graceless

Understanding and navigating personal triggers with a measure of mindfulness is an important part of adaptive and gracious behavior.

How much can we actually change? This question has been debated by people for a very long time. Experts from a variety of fields present us with a range of answers from "we have the power to change most everything" to "very little, if anything, is within our purview to change." Over the years of my work and study, I have moved closer to the latter answer. However, this does not mean I am a determinist or fatalist. I have personally experienced both my own transformation and adaptive behaviors in those I've coached and worked with. It remains a mystery to me why some of us, some of the time, seem to change. Yet most of us, a lot of the time, remain relatively static in our behaviors and attitudes.

Developmental psychology has revealed a mellowing that tends to occur with age. But does that really mean we are changing? We will leave this debate for another day. However, what is important for our discussion, no matter how much you believe you can change, is to appreciate and understand the situations, dynamics, and people that activate you. Along with other writers and thinkers, I call these activating situations, dynamics, and relationships, *triggers*.

As an individual member of a tribe, it is my responsibility to know the triggers that can activate my stress response in negative ways. Naming these triggers makes it more likely that I will be able to recognize them when they surface. The better I can see the trigger coming, the more possible it is to do something positive about it. The first step in all of this is to learn to identify your unique triggers.

Snapshot of a Trigger

My undergraduate degree is in music. Conducting is one skill that music majors develop during their studies. Whether it be conducting a choir, band, or orchestra (or something else), music majors learn the art of sending signals to a musical group through their hands, facial expressions, and bodily movements. These signals enable the musical tribe

166

to understand what the conductor wants at any given moment in the performance. As a music major, I spent a lot of time conducting recordings while standing in front of white walls in my dorm or apartment. However there was nothing like the moment when I was able to direct live human beings performing a musical piece. Conducting takes both know-how and confidence, both of which one is still acquiring at nineteen years of age and, for that matter, throughout one's life.

I will never forget one of the first times I conducted a choir that was *not* made up of other college students. The music director, at the church of my youth, gave me permission to join the choir for a rehearsal and conduct a choral piece the choir was learning. I can still see myself that day—my hands shaking, my mouth dry, and my nerves frazzled. I stood before the choir, a 19-year-old music major, trying to make my way through the composition. I missed several cues and, I'm sure, had a somewhat "sick to my stomach" look on my face.

At the end of the piece, the 100 adults in the choir showed kind support by clapping for me. I was pretty sure at that point I wouldn't throw up. Just as the kind gesture ended, the music director walked over to me and, in front of 100 adults, said to me, "That was pretty good, Dave, but now let me show you how it's really done." I froze in humiliation as I walked to the side of the room and watched him conduct the choir in what proved to be four of the longest minutes of my life. Back in my dorm later that night, I was mortified. I was shaken. It seems silly now, but it wasn't then. I questioned whether or not I should even be a music major. His simple words shot to the core of my insecurities and my hopes.

I was able to overcome this experience and continue my studies as well as my life. At 51, the incident seems trivial. But it has remained with me throughout my life and has contributed to one of my triggers. To this day, when I witness a person in positional power diminish another person who has less power, it infuriates me. I have found myself in numerous situations over the years where my own negative reactions were in part due to what I viewed as one person lording it over another. Ironically, as

I've confronted this type of person in coaching situations, I have, at times, treated the dominant person with the same dismissive power plays they applied to another person.

Snapshot of a Trigger (Here's Another One)

I've spent over 30 years speaking to groups of people. From the time I was a young adult to now, I have spoken to groups of thousands and groups of two or three. I enjoy few things more then the energy that comes from speaking to and connecting with an audience. Along the way, I discovered a very predictable and powerful trigger that overtakes me when I'm less than mindful. The trigger just happens to be a certain vibe I feel from audience members. When an audience is "with me," I experience tremendous energy from their engagement. However, when I notice a person or group of people seem disinterested in the moment, I am prone to frustration and anger. Blank stares and rigid body postures from audience members suggest to me that they are not engaged. In fact, it feels as if they are challenging me to engage them. Of course, these stares and postures could mean a thousand different things or mean nothing at all. This is all *my interpretation*, and my interpretation has often been wrong.

Over the years, I have done and said things while speaking—based on my assumption that someone was disengaged—that I wish I could've taken back. This trigger has certainly diminished the amount of alchemy I've brought to a presentation. My assumptions about the motives of listeners are nothing more than that, assumptions. But when I assign meaning to them (which I am very good at doing), they become personal affronts that can distract me from the very alchemy I'm trying to create, not to mention the judgments I'm heaping on a person in the audience.

Not all triggers are necessarily formed in childhood or as we perform specific activities. My examples are not meant to suggest that all triggers are the result of the negative actions (perceived or real) done to us. My stories only reveal that all of us come to our triggers through some kind of experience or preference. For example, perhaps we are introverted and are triggered by people who over-talk. Perhaps, on the other hand, we are extroverted and are triggered by people who remain silent. Perhaps we were treated a certain way during a very formative time of our lives and it has stayed with us. Now we are activated when treated in a similar fashion.

Perhaps one of our family members has a personality that clashes with our own, and when we find that type of person out in the world, it causes a reaction. Whatever the reasons that shape your triggers, it is important to understand their anatomy—first by noticing how the trigger may be connected to some experience or preference and then by naming them to understand, own, and frame the dynamics that occur when you experience them. For example, I am now very careful to watch what I say and do when I notice a person in a position of power become dominate toward another person or group of people. I want my words and actions to draw the dominant one into a safe space where he or she might be able to see another way. I have also developed strategies to notice and navigate those who appear to me to be disinterested when I'm speaking. All of this means that I must put the responsibility on myself to adjust my behavior. And that requires that I find the supports I need to minimize the activation and increase my grace under pressure.

Start here:

- Identify patterns in your activation. Do certain actions or situations consistently activate your biology and emotions in negative ways?
- Describe both the trigger (what activates you) and your reaction to it (your common behaviors in reaction to the trigger).
- Name the trigger.
- Notice when the trigger activates you.
- Minimize your reaction as much as possible (we will talk more about this in the next section).
- Develop the ability to read the arrival of the trigger early enough to avoid it or minimize it.

This takes a lifetime of work, and we often fail.

Get Scaffolding That Supports You

Once we know the triggers that activate us and make us less adaptive as tribe members, it's our personal responsibility to seek out the scaffolding support we need in order to minimize our negative activations. We considered the idea of scaffolding early in the book as a way to think about the Tribal Alchemy framework. The framework can support your tribe's ability to turn lesser into better. Here we use scaffolding as a way to think about the supports we individually need to minimize the effects of our activation points and dysfunctions (which also diminish the effectiveness of our tribe). Here are three types of scaffolding strategies that can help you minimize triggers and adapt more gracefully during difficulty.

Let's consider three types of scaffolding strategies and actions that you can take to utilize them.

Strategies of awareness building about triggers
- Notice the link between the trigger and your activation. Why do you think they are connected?
- Pay attention to dynamics occurring when the trigger arises.
- Find linkages from the current situation and past situations that have activated the trigger.
- Identify patterns in your activation. Do certain actions or situations consistently activate your biology and emotions in negative ways?
- Notice when the trigger activates you.
- Develop the ability to read the arrival of the trigger early enough to avoid it or minimize it. This takes a lifetime of work, and we often fail.

Strategies of action to diminish the power of the trigger
- Create a visual or word cue to remain mindful during times when triggers are most likely.
- Imagine yourself responding without activation during a trigger.

- Determine and practice activities that reduce activation when it occurs.
- Determine if any tribe members can be supportive and are willing to be during activation—coregulate each other.
- *Pause* when you've lost it.
- *Slow* when you're losing it.
- Increasing mindfulness when you see a trigger coming.

Strategies of tribal involvement
- Share your triggers with tribe members when you are not triggered (this requires trust).
- Alert tribe members when you are activated.
- Seek out wisdom on how to navigate triggers from trusted friends and advisors.
- Ask for help when you're activated. Sometimes other tribe members can talk us down or cover for us as we come down from a time of activation.

. . .

Finally, Adaptability Requires Regular Stretching

Watching me do yoga is not a pretty sight, although it is an amusing one. I've never been all that physically flexible. I've flirted with yoga and Pilates-like stretches for years. During many of these routines, my body feels like a two-by-four. Over the years, I've had teachers describe positions in which to put my body. Like a good two-by-four, I've tried. When I look at the teacher for confirmation of the move, there has often been a "Well, bless his heart" look on her face. That look has regularly confirmed my fear that I really am a two-by-four.

My inflexibility—and regular confirmation of it—has many times led me to make a decision that seals my fate. *I stop stretching.* I think, "I need to stop doing this because I just can't get it. I'm just not flexible." Of course, the irony is that the decision to stop stretching will only perpetuate inflexibility. The very activity that would make me more flexible is the very one I avoid.

One way to be more personally adaptable during times of challenge and opportunity is to stretch yourself (your nonphysical self) when you're not under pressure. This means orchestrating situations that will require you to stretch (metaphorically speaking) through discomfort. In other words, *create strategic discomfort that enables you to stretch*. The word "strategic" is important. I'm not suggesting you act irresponsibly so you can experience the awkward consequences of bad behavior. Instead, each of us has situations and circumstances we avoid or misappropriate because of rigidity or dysfunction. These uncomfortable situations and circumstances vary depending on our personalities, life narratives, and relationships. A situation that is a stretch for me may not be difficult for you. For instance, small dinner parties with unfamiliar people are difficult for me. You can put me in front of 5,000 people for a speaking engagement and I'm quite content, energized in fact. But if you put me in a room with a group of relatively unfamiliar people for a dinner party, I get uncomfortable in a hurry. As you can imagine, I avoid the dinner party because of the stretch it requires. But those dinner parties may actually make me more adaptable and pliable, if I attend one now and then. Not only does the dinner party require me to stretch, but it also gives me the opportunity to practice skills that don't come easy for me. This too can make me more adaptable in other situations, including situations with my tribe.

I have a friend who was asked to lead a retreat for an organization. Though the retreat fell within his skill set, some of the particulars of the retreat required him to study up on unfamiliar knowledge, as well as facilitate a process of discovery with the organization. This type of facilitation is not completely foreign to him, but he doesn't do it every day. As we talked about his experience, post-retreat, he said, "I'm really glad I did it. You know, I need to put myself in those kinds of situations now and then to stay sharp and develop myself." I agreed. Beyond self-development, his willingness to stretch will make him a better member of his own tribes.

Here are the steps to stretch yourself and enhance your adaptability:

First, in an awkward and uncomfortable situation, determine a strategy that will enhance flexibility

- Identify the situation.
- Find an opportunity to enter it.
- Think about a specific dysfunction you want to overcome during "the stretch." Name that dysfunction. For example, "I want to get better at _____." For example, take my dinner party woes. I might determine that I want to resist the lure of leaving because I feel _____.
- Determine a strategy that will enhance flexibility and enable you to practice a new behavior in the midst of the uncomfortable moment. Name that strategy or skill. For example, for my dinner party dysfunction I might try a strategy of refocusing my anxious energy on a meaningful conversation with another partygoer. Instead of leaving, I will focus on another. If you cannot think of a strategy, you may need to bounce the situation off another person who happens to be good at what you're seeking to stretch into.
- Stay long enough to feel your desire to run. Stay in the stretch long enough to feel *healthy* tension. Notice the feelings and thoughts that surface as you grow uncomfortable. Resist the temptation react mindlessly.
- Try the skill that helps you stay in the discomfort with more flexibility. Practice the strategy you crafted prior to entering the situation, even if it's just for a few minutes.
- Notice what happens to you as you practice.
- Debrief after with yourself and maybe another.

What did you learn?

- Did the strategy work?
- Did you feel a stretch?
- Do you think entering more uncomfortable situations would make you more adaptable?
- Rinse and repeat.

One final idea on stretching: In my limited attendance of yoga classes, I've heard teachers stress the importance of knowing your own body and the limits of what you can handle. This is about finding that zone of discomfort where the physical stretch is enough to challenge but not enough to harm you. The same concept applies to orchestrating the "stretches" to make you more adaptable. If the situations and circumstances you put yourself in are not challenging enough, the stretch will not yield more adaptive behaviors. But if the stretch is too difficult, it may harm you and create in you a distaste for any further stretching.

. . .

If individual tribe members don't adapt well, how will tribal alchemy suffer?

- Alchemy is lost without adaptation. In a word, *adaptation* describes what alchemy is and what occurs when it happens.
- Change is framed as death rather than life.
- Relationships grow stale.
- Scarcity mind-set (ironically) increases.
- Territorialism deepens.
- Hoarding replaces sharing.
- Leaders inhibit ingenuity out of fear.
- Tribal members inhibit ingenuity out of fear.
- Fear expands and shapes culture.
- Graciousness is lost.
- Tribal warfare replaces tribal connectivity.
- Suspicion colors tribal exchanges.